GRILLING
ESSENTIALS

**The All-in-One Guide to Firing Up
5-Star Meals with 130+ Recipes**

CRE▲TIVE
HOMEOWNER®

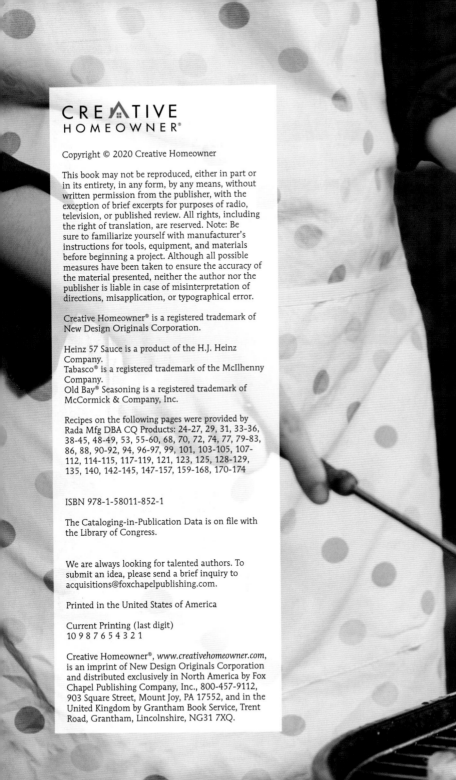

Recipes on the following pages were provided by Rada Mfg DBA CQ Products: 24-27, 29, 31, 33-36, 38-45, 48-49, 53, 55-60, 68, 70, 72, 74, 77, 79-83, 86, 88, 90-92, 94, 96-97, 99, 101, 103-105, 107-112, 114-115, 117-119, 121, 123, 125, 128-129, 135, 140, 142-145, 147-157, 159-168, 170-174

ISBN 978-1-58011-852-1

The Cataloging-in-Publication Data is on file with the Library of Congress.

We are always looking for talented authors. To submit an idea, please send a brief inquiry to acquisitions@foxchapelpublishing.com.

Printed in the United States of America

Current Printing (last digit)
10 9 8 7 6 5 4 3 2 1

Creative Homeowner®, *www.creativehomeowner.com*, is an imprint of New Design Originals Corporation and distributed exclusively in North America by Fox Chapel Publishing Company, Inc., 800-457-9112, 903 Square Street, Mount Joy, PA 17552, and in the United Kingdom by Grantham Book Service, Trent Road, Grantham, Lincolnshire, NG31 7XQ.

This book about the essentials of grilling is dedicated to everyone who enjoys the essentials of life: food, family and friends, and fun. Put on your apron, fire up the grill, and use these recipes to make delicious meals everyone will enjoy!

Contents

1 Pro Tips for a Grill-icious Meal

Grilling is really common sense. It's very simple. You should think of a grill as a burner—it just happens to have grates. You shouldn't be intimidated by it.
—Bobby Flay

ESSENTIAL GRILLING TIPS

The plans are made, the guests are coming soon, and you volunteered for Grill Master duties. Then you realize that a backyard barbecue party, a family reunion with grilled burgers and dogs, or an elegant, alfresco grilled dinner may be more than you bargained for. How hot should the grill be? How much time does it take to grill a steak? Should you try using wood chips to smoke the meat? Don't panic—read on! Here are some quick tips to help you become a true Grill Master with bragging rights.

PREP

✖ **Clean the grates** with a metal coil brush or scrub them with a ball of aluminum foil before cooking. This is especially important when cooking delicate foods, such as seafood or ground chicken patties.

✖ To **prevent food from sticking to the grate,** dip a folded paper towel in canola oil and rub it over grates until lightly coated with oil. If spraying grates with nonstick cooking spray, do it before lighting the grill. You may also brush meat and seafood lightly with olive oil before grilling.

WARNING! A metal bristle from a traditional wire bristle brush could break off and end up in your grilled food.

PREHEAT

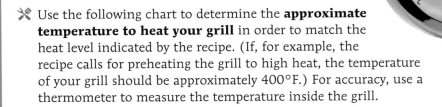

✂ **Preheat** a gas grill for 10 to 15 minutes before cooking. If using charcoal briquettes, light them and allow briquettes to turn white before placing food on the grate (it will take approximately 20 to 30 minutes).

✂ Use the following chart to determine the **approximate temperature to heat your grill** in order to match the heat level indicated by the recipe. (If, for example, the recipe calls for preheating the grill to high heat, the temperature of your grill should be approximately 400°F.) For accuracy, use a thermometer to measure the temperature inside the grill.

High heat	400°F
Medium-high heat	375°F
Medium heat	350°F
Medium-low heat	325°F
Low heat	300°F

GRILL

✂ **If making kebabs or grilling small pieces of food,** thread food on metal skewers, or use wooden skewers that have been soaked in water for 15 to 30 minutes to prevent scorching. The food will twist less if threaded on a pair of skewers.

✂ **Trim off excess fat** from steaks, chops and roasts before grilling to prevent flare-ups. Cut off excess poultry skin before marinating or cooking.

✂ **Mix seasonings into ground meats** before grilling, using hands as needed.

✂ When making ground meat patties, gently **shape the meat with a fork** to avoid compressing the meat too firmly.

✂ **Use a spatula or tongs to turn meats** such as chicken breasts or steaks. Avoid forks, which pierce the meat and cause juices to run out.

✂ **Soak meats in a brine or marinade** to increase flavor and juiciness.

✂ **If basting meats with melted butter,** avoid flare-ups by grilling one side first and turning the meat over before brushing with butter.

✂ **Clean the grates well before cooking sides and sweets.** You don't want your pineapple to taste like a ribeye.

✂ When using **saucepans or bakeware on the grill,** keep in mind the bottom may get charred. Be sure to use heat-proof cast iron, stainless steel or disposable foil pans.

FOOD SAFETY TIPS

✖ **Wash hands and cutting boards** thoroughly after handling raw meat or poultry. Never place cooked meats on the same surface previously used to hold raw meats unless it has been washed well.

✖ On picnics, **use well-insulated coolers and ice packs** to keep foods cold and prevent bacteria growth before and after cooking (40°F or below).

✖ **Serve grilled foods hot, and chill leftovers** as soon as the meal is over.

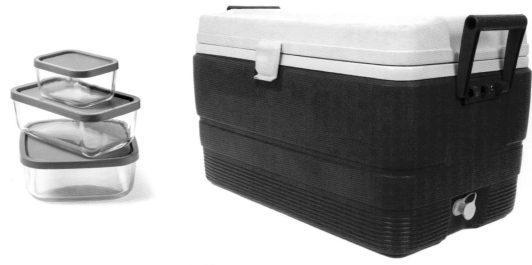

GAS VS. CHARCOAL

Most dishes can be prepared equally well on a gas or charcoal grill, allowing you to enjoy all kinds of recipes using the equipment you have on hand.

Grilling without a lid on a charcoal grill may require a slight increase in temperature and cooking time. Grilling food with the lid on can enhance the grilled flavor and shorten the cooking time, even with a slightly lower temperature.

To change the temperature of a charcoal grill, use fewer coals to reduce the heat or add more briquettes around the edges to make it hotter. The grate of the grill may also be moved closer or further from the heat source to increase or decrease the heat.

Gas grills usually have a built-in temperature gauge and dials to regulate the heat and number of burners turned on, but check the accuracy of that gauge before relying on it. A barbeque-safe oven thermometer may be more accurate.

Flare-ups occur when fats/oils drip on the heat source. To extinguish flames on a charcoal grill, squirt water on them. On a gas grill, just close the lid to remove the source of air.

Kebabs on a charcoal grill

Kebabs on a gas grill

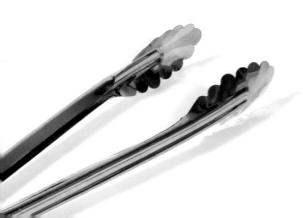

Propane tank ready for grilling

DIRECT OR INDIRECT HEAT?

When food is placed on the grate right over the heat source, it will cook quickly by **direct heat**. This is best for small, tender foods that can be cooked in less than 30 minutes. The grill does not need a lid unless otherwise directed.

To cook foods more slowly, use **indirect heat**. This is accomplished by heating only one section of the grill and placing the food on the grate over the remaining cooler section before closing the lid. The heat will circulate inside the grill to cook the food slowly at a lower temperature ("low and slow"). Avoid opening the lid to peek at the food. It is best to use a thermometer to measure the temperature inside the grill when cooking this way.

To lock in the juices of larger cuts of meat, sear all sides over hot direct heat for 1 to 2 minutes per side. Then reduce the heat, close the lid and move the food on the grate as needed to finish cooking over direct or indirect heat.

Placing an aluminum drip pan (holding a small amount of water) in the bottom of the grill also reduces flare-ups and provides moisture for indirect cooking. The pan should be set underneath the cooking area, with heat surrounding the pan.

After cooking on any grill, burn off residue on the grates and when cool, scrape off baked-on food before putting the grill away.

Steak cooking over direct heat

Thick pork chops cooking over indirect heat

WOOD CHIPS & SMOKING

To get a smoked flavor in grilled meats, add fully dried (not green) wood chunks or chips to the charcoal or gas grill before cooking. Fruit woods, such as apple, plum or cherry, complement turkey. Hickory is a good choice for almost any type of meat, especially pork. Mesquite works well if used sparingly. Wood chunks tend to smolder rather than burn, which produces steadier smoke than chips. Never use treated lumber scraps or wood from high-sap trees like pine or fir, though cedar planks can be used to smoke salmon on the grill.

Soak one or two handfuls of the wood in water for 1 hour and then drain well. In a charcoal grill, place the damp wood directly on the briquettes, around the outer edges. In either a charcoal or gas grill, wood can also be placed in a smoke box, small disposable foil pan or a heavy-duty foil pouch poked full of holes. Set this container on the lava rocks in a gas grill or directly on the charcoal before preheating, locating it near the back or to one side of the grill. When the grill is hot and smoke is produced, reduce the grill's temperature and place meat on the grate away from the smoke. (Never place meat directly over the smoke.) Close the lid and let the smoke seep into the meat as it cooks. If food requires a long grilling time, add more wood as needed, especially during the first two hours of cooking.

Soaking mesquite wood chips before smoking meat on a grill

MORE GRILLING METHODS

✗ Use a **grill basket** to keep food from slipping through the grates and for ease in turning food during grilling. The food won't stick to the grill, and you don't have to deal with tongs or turners, especially if the basket has heat-safe handles.

✗ **Grilling in foil** keeps moisture in the food and saves on clean-up. Use heavy-duty aluminum foil or two or three layers of regular-weight foil to prevent rips and help protect food from high temperatures. Use potholders and long tongs to handle foil packets, and support packets with a baking sheet when moving to and from the grill. Remember, contents will be hot, so use caution when opening the packet.

✗ Using **skewers** helps to hold foods together during grilling. Cut foods into bite-size pieces for quick and easy grilling and use heavy-duty stainless steel or wooden skewers. Wooden skewers should be soaked in water for about 30 minutes before using to prevent burning. Some foods benefit from using two skewers, side by side, to keep the food from turning and slipping.

Lamb chops in a grill basket

Foil packets on a grill

Skewers used to make kebabs on the grill

TEMPERATURE GUIDE FOR GRILLED MEATS

Meats and seafood should be cooked thoroughly for safe eating. Cooking times in the recipes are approximate. The time required may vary due to the size and shape of the food, personal preferences and the weather. In cool or windy weather, it may be necessary to cook food longer.

Use of an instant-read thermometer can prevent under- or over-cooking. Insert it in the thickest part of the cut to obtain an accurate reading. Though all meats and seafood must be grilled to safe minimum internal temperatures before serving, you may prefer to cook some cuts to a higher temperature. However, over-cooking causes meat and seafood to dry out. Remember that foods will continue to cook for a few minutes after being removed from the grill.

A thermometer is an important tool when grilling meat.

USDA guidelines recommend cooking foods to the following minimum internal temperatures to kill harmful food bacteria.

MEAT	TEMPERATURE
Fish	145°
Beef Roasts and Steaks	145°F (rare) 160°F (medium) 170°F (well-done)
Ground Beef and Ground Pork	160°F
Pork Chops, Tenderloins, Roasts	145°F
Ground Poultry	165°F
Chicken Breasts	165°F (up to 170°F)
Chicken or Turkey Thighs, Legs, Quarters, Whole Birds	165°F (up to 180°F)

Tender or thin cuts of meat can be placed directly over higher heat to be grilled quickly (less than 30 minutes). Cuts of meat that are tougher or larger need to be cooked more slowly, using lower temperatures and moisture to become tender. It is also helpful to soak these cuts in a tenderizing marinade before grilling.

Many meats benefit from resting or standing time. After removing meat from the grill, cover with a foil tent and let stand for 5 to 15 minutes before slicing. This allows the internal temperature to rise adequately and juices to redistribute throughout the meat.

Q: "HOW LONG DO I COOK IT?"
A: "UNTIL IT'S DONE."

The only honest answer is that you need to learn from experience. Outdoor temperature, humidity, wind conditions, the thickness and type of meat, and the equipment you're using all factor into the finished product. Use the cooking times given in this book as a guide, and apply the USDA guidelines for safe internal food temperatures. Remember, however, that most cuts of meat will continue to cook after they are removed from the heat, rising an additional 5°F to 10°F.

QUICK GUIDE TO MARINADES, SAUCES, HERBS, RUBS, GLAZES & BRINES

MARINADES & BRINES

Marinades and brines add flavor, moisture and tenderness to meats and seafood before grilling. If you wish to brush meat with some of the marinade during grilling, it is best to reserve a portion of the mixture before using the remaining mixture to soak raw meat. Marinade that has been in contact with raw meat may contain bacteria that could contaminate the cooked meat. The used marinade should be boiled for at least 3 minutes before being used on cooked meat.

There are two good methods to marinate meat and seafood. For quick clean-ups, place the food in a large heavy-duty resealable plastic bag resting in a large bowl. Pour the marinade over the food, seal the bag and gently turn it until meat or seafood is well coated. Alternatively, use a non-reactive container, such as a shallow glass baking dish or stainless steel or plastic bowl (never aluminum). Place the meat in the container, pour marinade over the top, turn the pieces several times until well coated and then cover the dish. Always refrigerate meat or seafood while it marinates and turn it several times to incorporate flavors.

To cook, remove food from the plastic bag or dish and discard the marinade. Do not rinse off the marinade, but if the meat seems too wet, pat off the excess

Using a marinade for chicken before grilling

Chicken wings soaking in brine

with paper towels. This prevents the marinade from dripping into the grill and causing flare-ups. Use the fresh reserved marinade to baste the meat or seafood as it cooks. Reserved marinade can also be served alongside the grilled food.

Marinades with an acidic ingredient, like vinegar, wine or citrus juice, help tenderize meat or seafood. Avoid marinades with too many sweet ingredients as they can cause the meat to burn.

Brines are typically salty soaks and are not used for basting or serving. Always discard the brine after soaking is complete, and rinse the meat before grilling to remove excess salt. Though brining will shorten the cooking time, it turns pork and beef gray in color, so it's best to grill meat thoroughly for a nicely browned appearance.

RUBS

Dry rubs are combinations of spices and seasonings without any wet ingredients. These rubs increase a meat's natural browning. Wet rubs are paste-like because oil or another wet ingredient is mixed in with the spices and seasonings to create a crust.

Apply a rub 15 to 20 minutes before grilling so the seasonings can penetrate into the meat. Sprinkle the rub mixture over the meat or seafood and gently pat or massage it in with your fingers. Avoid rubbing the mixture into the meat too vigorously.

Standard rub seasonings include salt and pepper. For best results, choose coarse kosher salt, which won't create a wet surface on meat like table salt can, and use freshly ground black pepper, whose oils offer a deeper flavor. Brown sugar will add more flavor than white sugar in sweet rubs.

If meat has been soaked in a brine or salty marinade, rinse the meat and use a salt-free rub before grilling.

Dry rub on chicken legs

SALSAS & RELISHES

Salsas and relishes made from fruits or vegetables add color, flavor and texture to grilled dishes. When served chilled, they also offer a nice temperature contrast. Whether chunky or almost smooth, salsas

Fresh tomato salsa—yum!

Basting chicken on the grill

and relishes can be spooned on top or served alongside grilled poultry, beef, pork or seafood. Choose fresh seasonal ingredients that complement the flavor of the grilled meat or seafood.

SAUCES & GLAZES

Sauces and glazes are used to baste meats as they cook on the grill, and they can also be served over grilled dishes. If there is a high sugar content in the sauce or glaze, wait until the end of the cooking time before brushing the meat with it. This prevents burning and allows the sauce to caramelize before serving. If using the mixture as both a basting sauce and finishing sauce, you must boil it for several minutes before serving. A "mop" is a thin barbeque sauce brushed on food like ribs during grilling. It adds flavor and keeps food moist.

You can always have fresh herbs handy by growing your own.

HERBS

Some recipes call for fresh herbs while others may ask for dried. If you don't have the type requested in the recipe, you can simply replace it with another form. Use these approximate equivalents to help determine how much to use: 1 tablespoon finely cut fresh herbs = 1 teaspoon crumbled dried herbs = ¼ to ½ teaspoon ground dried herbs

2 Poultry

I grill, therefore I am.
—*Alton Brown*

POULTRY
COOKING TIPS

Fully cooked poultry should reach the internal temperatures listed below, as shown by a thermometer. Grilled chicken or turkey is generally done when the meat is no longer pink inside and the juices run clear when sliced in the thickest part.

Boneless skinless chicken breast halves and tenders:	165° to 170°F
Chicken parts: wings, legs, thighs, quarters:	165° to 180°F
Whole chicken:	165° to 180°F
Boneless skinless turkey tenderloin steaks:	165° to 170°F
Turkey drumsticks:	165° to 179°F
Ground chicken and turkey:	165°F

BASIC GRILLED CHICKEN BREASTS

MAKES 4 SERVINGS

- ❯ 4 boneless skinless chicken breast halves
- ❯ 1 (16 oz.) bottle Italian salad dressing
- ❯ Lemon pepper to taste
- ❯ Salt to taste

Rinse chicken breast halves and pat dry. Place chicken in a large resealable plastic bag and pour salad dressing over the chicken. Seal bag and turn several times to coat meat. Refrigerate bag to marinate chicken for 2 to 3 hours, turning twice to marinate evenly.

To cook, lightly oil the grate and preheat grill to medium heat. Remove chicken breasts from bag and discard marinade. Arrange chicken on the grate directly over heat and season with lemon pepper and salt. Cook for 12 to 15 minutes, turning once halfway through cooking and adjusting heat as needed for even grilling. When meat is no longer pink and juices run clear, place chicken breasts on a serving plate and cover with foil to rest for 5 to 10 minutes, allowing internal temperature to reach 165° to 170°F before serving.

Note: Boneless skinless chicken breast halves cook quickly on a grill, but cooking time depends on the size and thickness of each piece. Generally, if using medium direct heat, they will need approximately 12 to 15 minutes, turning once partway through cooking. If using indirect heat, allow about 5 minutes longer.

GRILLED CHICKEN TENDERS

MAKES 6 SERVINGS

- 1 ½ lbs. chicken tenders (or boneless chicken breast cut into strips)
- ½ C. buttermilk
- Salt and black pepper to taste

Wash chicken tenders and pat dry. In a large resealable plastic bag, combine chicken tenders and buttermilk. Seal bag and turn several times until chicken is well coated. Refrigerate to marinate tenders for 1 hour.

To cook, lightly oil the grate and preheat grill to medium-high heat. Remove chicken from bag, drain and pat dry. Discard marinade. Season chicken tenders with salt and pepper. Arrange chicken on the grate over heat and cook for 5 to 6 minutes, turning once partway through cooking. Remove from grill when meat is no longer pink, juices run clear an internal temperature reaches 165° to 170°F.

CHIPOTLE CHICKEN FAJITAS

MAKES 5 SERVINGS

- 1 (12 oz.) bottle chili sauce
- ¼ C. lime juice
- 4 chipotle peppers in adobo sauce (or to taste)
- 1 lb. chicken tenders, sliced into thin strips
- ½ C. cider vinegar
- ⅓ C. brown sugar
- ⅓ C. molasses
- 4 green bell peppers, cut into 1" pieces
- 1 onion, cut into 1" pices
- 1 T. olive oil
- ⅛ tsp. salt
- ⅛ tsp. black pepper
- 10 (8") flour tortillas
- 1½ C. chopped tomatoes
- 1 C. shredded Mexican cheese blend

In a food processor, combine chili sauce, lime juice and chipotle peppers; cover and process until blended. Transfer ½ cup of mixture to a large resealable plastic bag. Add chicken tenders, seal bag and turn to coat well. Refrigerate bag to marinate chicken for 1 to 4 hours. Pour remaining marinade into a small bowl. Add vinegar, brown sugar and molasses; mix well. Cover and refrigerate.

To cook, lightly oil the grate and preheat grill to medium heat. On six metal or soaked wooden skewers, alternately thread pieces of chicken, green pepper and onion. Brush with oil and sprinkle with salt and black pepper. Place on the grate and cover grill; cook for 10 to 16 minutes, turning occasionally, or until chicken is no longer pink inside and juices run clear. Remove chicken and vegetables from skewers and place in a large bowl. Add ½ cup chipotle-molasses mixture and toss to coat; keep warm. Grill tortillas, uncovered, over medium heat for 45 to 55 seconds on each side or until warmed. Top each tortilla with a portion of the chicken mixture, tomatoes, cheese and remaining chipotle-molasses mixture; roll up and serve.

GRILLED CHICKEN WINGS

MAKES 8 TO 10 SERVINGS

- 4 lbs. chicken wings (20 to 24 wings)
- 3 T. Olive oil
- 2 tsp. salt
- Bottled sauce of choice (BBQ or hot sauce)

Rinse chicken wings and pat dry. Separate each wing at the joint to make two pieces. Cut off and discard wing tips.

Lightly oil the grate and preheat grill to medium heat. Place remaining wing sections in a large bowl and drizzle with olive oil. Sprinkle with salt and work chicken pieces with hands until evenly coated.

To cook, arrange wings on the grate, cover grill and cook for 20 to 30 minutes or until tender and cooked through, turning occasionally. Juices should run clear and internal temperature in the thickest part should reach 165° to 180°F. Remove from the grill and serve with sauce on the side for dipping, or coat grilled wings in the sauce before serving with additional dip.

SPICED CRANBERRY WINGS

MAKES 4 SERVINGS

- 3 to 4 lbs. chicken wings
- 1 C. balsamic vinaigrette dressing
- 1 (14-oz.) can jellied cranberry sauce
- 2 T. Tabasco sauce
- ½ tsp. salt
- ¼ tsp. pepper

Remove and discard tips from chicken wings. Combine remaining ingredients in a bowl, and whisk with a fork until smooth. Refrigerate half of the sauce to serve with the cooked wings.

Put the chicken and the remaining sauce in a resealable plastic bag; shake to coat well; and refrigerate from 3 hours to overnight.

Preheat grill to medium. Remove chicken from the marinade, and place on the grill skin side down. Discard marinade. Cook wings for about 10 to 12 minutes per side, basting often with the reserved sauce. Serve hot with remaining dipping sauce.

COCONUT CHICKEN WINGS

MAKES 6 TO 8 SERVINGS

- 3 lbs. chicken wings (15 to 18 wings)
- 3 T. olive oil
- 2 T. soy sauce
- 2 T. sugar
- 1 tsp. curry powder
- ½ tsp. salt
- ¼ tsp. black pepper
- ½ tsp. grated lemon peel
- 1 C. coconut milk
- 1 C. sweetened flaked coconut

Rinse chicken wings and separate each wing at the joint to make two pieces. Cut off and discard wing tips. In a large bowl, whisk together oil, soy sauce, sugar, curry powder, salt, black pepper and lemon peel. Add coconut milk and whisk until blended. Reserve ½ cup of the mixture and divide it evenly between two small containers; refrigerate for basting and serving later. To remaining mixture, add chicken wings; toss until well coated. Cover and refrigerate to marinate wings for at least 1 hour or overnight.

Before grilling, heat a medium skillet over medium heat. Add coconut and toast for about 10 minutes of until golden brown, stirring constantly. Transfer toasted coconut to a plate to cool. Lightly crumble the flakes with fingers and set aside.

To cook, lightly oil the grates and preheat grill to medium heat. Remove wings from bowl and discard marinade. Arrange wings on the grate, baste with one container of reserved marinade and grill the wings for 8 to 10 minutes. Turn, baste again and cook for 8 to 10 minutes more or until meat is no longer pink. As wings finish cooking, transfer remaining reserved marinade to a small saucepan and heat thoroughly. Transfer the cooked wings to a platter and coat them with the warmed marinade. Sprinkle wings with toasted coconut and serve immediately.

HONEY BBQ WINGS

MAKES 2 SERVINGS

- 10 whole chicken wings
- ¼ C. dry BBQ rub

HONEY BBQ SAUCE
- 1 C. ketchup

- ½ C. local honey
- ½ C. brown sugar
- 2 T. apple cider vinegar
- 1½ T. Worcestershire sauce

- ¾ tsp. kosher salt
- ¾ tsp. black pepper
- ¾ tsp. chili powder
- ¼ tsp. dried minced garlic
- ¼ tsp. dried onion flake

Take the wings out of the packaging and wipe them dry. Place the wings on a rack and place in the refrigerator to air dry for one hour. This step is optional but gives you the crispiest crust.

Preheat the grill to 375°F–400°F (medium high). Stir together all the Honey BBQ Sauce ingredients in a medium pot over medium high heat. Bring to a simmer and cook for 5 minutes to let the flavors blend. Taste for seasoning and add a pinch or two of salt and pepper as desired.

Season the wings on all sides with the dry BBQ rub. Place the wings top side down on the grate and cook, flipping every 5 minutes, until the wings reach an internal temperature of 180°F, about 20–25 minutes. Keep the lid closed when you aren't actively handling the wings.

Brush some of the Honey BBQ Sauce on all sides of the wings. Cook just long enough for the sauce to "set" on the wings, about 1 minute per side. The sauce will burn so keep a very close watch at this point. Using the upper rack of your grill (if equipped) makes this a bit easier so you can see when it's time to flip and the heat is less intense. Remove and serve with the remaining Honey BBQ Sauce on the side.

BEER-BRINED GRILLED CHICKEN

MAKES 4 SERVINGS

- 2 T. coarse salt
- 2 T. brown sugar
- 2 (12 oz.) cans regular or non-alcoholic beer, chilled
- 1 (3 to 3½ lb.) whole fryer chicken, quartered
- 1½ tsp. paprika
- ½ tsp. salt
- ¼ tsp. onion powder
- ¼ tsp. garlic powder
- ¼ tsp. black pepper
- 2 T. vegetable oil

In a 6- to 8-quart non-corrosive container (stainless steel, enamel-coated or plastic), combine 1 cup water with coarse salt and brown sugar, stirring until salt and sugar dissolve. Stir in beer. Add chicken, cover and refrigerate for 8 to 24 hours.

One hour before cooking, line a 9 x 13-inch baking pan with aluminum foil. Remove chicken from beer brine and discard brine. Rinse chicken with cool water and pat dry. Place chicken in pan and refrigerate uncovered for 1 hour to dry chicken skin. Meanwhile, in a small bowl, combine paprika, salt, onion powder, garlic powder and black pepper; mix well and set aside.

To cook, lightly oil the grate and preheat grill to medium heat, preparing it for indirect cooking. Brush oil over chicken and sprinkle with paprika mixture. Place chicken on the grate above the unheated side or over indirect heat and drip pan. Cover grill and cook for 15 minutes. Turn chicken, cover grill and cook for 20 to 30 minutes longer, turning occasionally until juices run clear and internal temperature reaches 165° to 170°F in the breast meat and 165° to 180°F in the thigh.

EASY BBQ CHICKEN

- 2 T. paprika
- 2 T. cumin
- 1 T. kosher salt
- 1 T. chili powder
- ½ T. allspice
- 4 chicken thighs, bone-in, skin-on
- ½ C. barbecue sauce

Mix the paprika, cumin, salt, chili powder and allspice together and liberally coat the chicken on both sides. Let it sit in refrigerator for 1 hour or more. Preheat your gas grill on high, with the lid down, for 10–15 minutes.

Once preheated, turn down the burners to medium-high. Place the thighs on the grates and grill on one side for about seven minutes or until the meat naturally releases from the grill. You can check if the chicken is ready by lifting up a corner of the thigh. If it resists and sticks, then let it grill for another few minutes before you try again. Once you can easily lift the chicken off the grill, flip and repeat the process on the second side, but with the lid closed.

After seven minutes or so, once the chicken releases easily from the grill, move all the thighs onto one half of your grill. Turn off the burner directly under the chicken, but leave the other burner or burners on. Close the lid. Cook the chicken for another 10 minutes, then lift the lid and brush the tops lightly with barbecue sauce.

Cook for another 10 minutes until your chicken is done—when it reads at least 165°F on your thermometer. Use the rack above the grill to put your chicken on if it's cooking too fast or too hot.

GRILLED CHICKEN ON A CAN

MAKES 6 SERVINGS

- 1 T. paprika
- 2 tsp. salt
- ½ tsp. garlic powder
- ½ tsp. onion powder
- ½ tsp. black pepper
- 1 (4–4½ lb) whole chicken
- 1 (12 oz.) can regular or non-alcoholic beer

For best results, use a charcoal rill with a drip pan placed directly under the grilling area. Add a small amount of water to pan. Arrange hot coals around the edge of the drip pan. If using a gas grill, use medium indirect heat.

In a small bowl, mix paprika, salt, garlic powder, onion powder and black pepper. Rinse chicken and pat dry. Fold wings of chicken across back with tips touching. Sprinkle paprika mixture inside chicken cavity and over outside of chicken; rub with fingers. Remove ½ cup of beer from the can. Holding chicken upright, with opening of body cavity down, insert beer can into cavity so chicken sits over can.

To cook, place chicken and can upright on the grate over the drip pan (or over unheated side of gas grill). Cover grill and cook for 1¼ to 1½ hours or until juices run clear, and the internal temperature of thigh meat reaches 165° to 180°F. Using tongs and a large sturdy spatula under the can, carefully lift chicken and can off the grate and place it in a 9 x 13-inch pan. Let stand for 15 minutes before removing can and carving chicken. Discard can.

GINGER PEACH-GLAZED CHICKEN

MAKES 6 SERVINGS

- 1 (4 to 5 lb) whole chicken
- Salt and black pepper to taste
- ½ C. peach preserves, large pieces chopped
- 1 T. white wine vinegar

- 1 T. prepared horseradish
- 1 tsp. freshly grated ginger
- ½ tsp. salt
- ½ tsp. coarsely ground black pepper

For best results use a charcoal grill with a drip pan placed directly under the grilling area. Add a small amount of water to the drip pan and arrange hot coals around the edge of the pan. If using a gas grill, use medium indirect heat.

Rinse chicken and pat dry. Pull the neck sin to the back and fasten with a short skewer. Tie drumsticks to tail with string. Fold wings of chicken across back with tips touching. Season with salt and pepper inside chicken cavity and over outside of chicken; rub with fingers.

To cook, place chicken on the grate over indirect heat, breast side up. Cover grill and cook for 1 hour. Cut string between drumsticks, cover and cook for 45 to 60 minutes more or until juices run clear and internal temperature of thigh meat reaches 165° to 180°F.

Near the end of the cooking time, prepare glaze. In a small microwave-safe bowl, combine peach preserves, vinegar, horseradish, ginger, salt and black pepper. Stir well and microwave on high power for 30 to 60 seconds or until preserves are melted, stirring once. Brush preserves mixture over chicken several times during the last 15 minutes of grilling. Transfer chicken to a serving platter, cover loosely with foil and let stand 15 minutes before carving.

TACO CHICKEN BURGERS

MAKES 4 SERVINGS

- 1 lb. uncooked ground chicken
- ½ small onion, diced
- 1 tsp. minced garlic
- ½ (1 oz.) pkg. dry taco seasoning mix
- 1 egg, lightly beaten
- ½ C. dry bread crumbs
- Salt and black pepper to taste
- Hamburger buns, split
- Condiments: pepper-jack cheese, avocado slices, chopped jalapeno peppers, salsa

Lightly oil the grate and preheat grill to medium heat. In a large bowl, combine chicken, onion, garlic, taco seasoning, egg and bread crumbs; mix well, using hands as needed. Season with salt and black pepper. Shape mixture into four soft patties, about ½ inch thick. Place patties on the grate, cover grill and cook for 10 to 16 minutes, turning once, until internal temperature reaches 165°F. Serve on buns topped with cheese, avocado, jalapeno peppers and salsa.

THAI
TURKEY BURGERS

MAKES 4 SERVINGS

- 1 egg, beaten
- ¼ C. fine dry bread crumbs
- 1 tsp. Thai seasoning or curry powder
- 1 lb. uncooked ground turkey breast
- 4 whole grain hamburger buns, split
- ¼ C. fresh basil leaves
- 2 T. peanut sauce
- 1 medium mango, pitted, peeled and sliced

Lightly oil the grate and preheat grill to medium heat. In a medium bowl, combine egg, bread crumbs and Thai seasoning. Add ground turkey and mix well. Shape into four soft patties, about ¾ inch thick. Place patties on the grate and cook for 14 to 18 minutes, turning once, until internal temperature reaches 165°F. To serve, place a few basil leaves on the bottom half of the bun, add patties and spoon peanut sauce over patties. Top with mango slices and bun tops.

BBQ SMOKED TURKEY WINGS

MAKES 2 SERVINGS

› 6 turkey wings › Favorite BBQ sauce › Cherry wood chips

Segment the turkey wings by cutting at the joints. Discard the wing tips. Marinate the wings in your favorite BBQ sauce from anywhere between 2–24 hours. If using a grill, set up heat for indirect grilling and place a smoker box with wood chips. Add the turkey wings to the other side of the grill. Let smoke until internal temperature reaches 165°F. Use your digital meat thermometer to be sure.

BUFFALO CHICKEN HAND PIES

MAKES 8 SERVINGS

> 2 boneless chicken breast halves, cubed and cooked
> ½ C. wing sauce
> 8 oz. shredded Pepper Jack cheese

> 4 oz. shredded cheddar cheese
> ⅓ C. ranch dressing
> Salt and black pepper to taste
> 1 (14.1 oz.) pkg. refrigerated pie crusts

Stir together chicken, wing sauce, both cheeses, ⅓ cup dressing, salt, and pepper. Cut each pie crust into three 5½- to 6-inch circles. Put a little of the chicken mixture over each circle, leaving ¼ inch along edge. Dampen edges of dough with water, fold circle in half, and crimp with a fork. Wrap in foil; chill or freeze.

GRILLED TEQUILA CHICKEN

MAKES 4 SERVINGS

- 4 boneless, skinless chicken breasts
- ⅓ C. lime juice
- 2 T. jalapeño pepper jelly
- 2 T. fresh chopped cilantro
- 2 T. tequila
- 2 T. olive oil
- 1 tsp. fresh minced garlic
- ¼ tsp. salt
- ¼ tsp. pepper

Rinse chicken breasts and pat dry. Arrange chicken breasts in an 8-inch square baking dish and set aside. In a small bowl, combine lime juice, jalapeño pepper jelly, fresh chopped cilantro, tequila, olive oil, minced garlic, salt, and pepper. Mix well and pour over chicken in baking dish. Cover baking dish and let marinate in refrigerator 2 to 8 hours. Preheat grill to medium-high heat. Place marinated chicken over grill and heat until chicken is cooked through.

CHICKEN SALAD BOATS

MAKES 18 SERVINGS

- 4 packages of precooked chicken tenders (about 20 per package)
- 18 hard rolls
- 3 C. finely chopped celery
- 1 medium onion, peeled and finely chopped
- 4 T. mayonnaise
- 1 large bottle Italian salad dressing
- Salt and pepper to taste
- 18 slices provolone cheese

Preheat grill to medium heat and cover the grate with aluminum foil. Grill chicken tenders until heated through, remove from grill, and cut into small pieces. Meanwhile, hollow out hard rolls by cutting a hole in the top of each roll and pulling out the bread, leaving bottom intact to make a boat shape. In a medium bowl, combine chicken tender pieces, chopped celery, chopped onion, mayonnaise, Italian salad dressing, salt, and pepper. Mix well and spoon mixture into hollowed rolls. Place rolls in a metal 9 x 13-inch baking dish. Place a slice of provolone cheese over each roll in baking dish. Place baking dish over heated grill until cheese melts and rolls are slightly browned. Remove from grill and serve warm.

CHICKEN ALFREDO PIZZAS

MAKES 4 SERVINGS

- 2 C. bread flour
- 1½ tsp. sugar
- 1 (.25 oz.) pkg. active dry yeast
- ¾ tsp. salt
- ¾ C. warm water (110°F)
- Olive oil
- ½ (14.5 oz.) jar Alfredo sauce (we used roasted garlic parmesan)

- 2 Roma tomatoes, finely diced
- 1 green bell pepper, finely diced
- ½ small onion, finely diced
- 6 oz. chicken breast, grilled
- 1 C. finely shredded mozzarella cheese
- ½ C. baby spinach, chopped
- Grated Parmesan cheese
- Coarse black pepper

Stir together the flour, sugar, yeast, and salt in the bowl of a stand mixer. Using a dough hook with the mixer running, add the water and 1 tablespoon plus 1 teaspoon oil, and beat until the dough forms a ball. Continue to beat for 5 minutes, until the dough is nice and smooth; transfer to an oiled bowl, cover with plastic wrap, and let rest for 20 minutes. You can use the dough now or chill up to 24 hours (then let warm to room temperature before rolling out).

Preheat the grill on low heat. Flatten the dough into a large rectangle on a floured flat cookie sheet, then transfer to a well-greased grill pan, patting to fit. Score with a knife into four rectangles. Cook until the bottom is nicely browned and the dough is firm enough to flip. Remove the pan from the grill, cut dough on the score lines, and flip the dough over. Brush the edges of the crusts with oil. Spread sauce to within ½ inch of the edges.

Divide the tomatoes, bell pepper, onion, chicken, mozzarella, and spinach among the crusts and sprinkle liberally with Parmesan and black pepper. Return the pan to the grill, close the lid, and heat until the dough is cooked, the cheese is melted, and everything is nice and warm.

TURKEY-APPLE MEATBALLS

MAKES 8 SERVINGS

> 1 C. barbecue sauce
> ½ C. grape jelly
> 4 tsp. apple cider vinegar
> ½ C. chicken stock

> 2 red apples
> ½ lb. uncooked bacon, finely chopped
> 2 lbs. ground turkey
> 1 ½ tsp. salt

Grease the grill grate and preheat the grill on low heat. In a saucepan, whisk together BBQ sauce, grape jelly, apple cider vinegar, and chicken stock. Set the saucepan on the grill to slowly warm up. Shred the unpeeled red apples onto heavy-duty paper towels and squeeze out the excess juice; dump the apples into a bowl. Add finely chopped, uncooked bacon, ground turkey, and salt; mix with your hands until evenly combined. Use a 2-inch cookie scoop to form meatballs and thread onto side-by-side thick skewers. Grill 35 to 45 minutes, until cooked through, turning and drizzling with the warmed sauce occasionally. Serve the remaining sauce with the meatballs.

SWEET SOUTHERN DRUMSTICKS

MAKES 12 SERVINGS

- ¼ C. brown sugar
- 2 tsp. minced garlic
- 4 tsp. salt
- 2 tsp. black pepper

- 12 chicken drumsticks
- ½ C. of your favorite sweet BBQ sauce
- 3 T. pure maple syrup
- 2 T. ketchup

In a zippered plastic bag, mash together the brown sugar, garlic, salt, and black pepper to form a paste. Toss in the drumsticks, seal the bag, and rub thoroughly until the chicken is coated. Chill overnight. Grease the grill grate and preheat the grill on medium heat for indirect cooking. Whisk together the BBQ sauce, syrup, and ketchup and set aside. Arrange the drumsticks on the hot side of the grill, cooking until browned on all sides. Then move them over to the cool side and cook 30 minutes longer, until the internal temperature of the chicken reaches 165°F, basting with the sauce several times near the end of cooking.

BBQ CHICKEN SKILLET DIP

SERVES A CROWD

- 2 8-oz. blocks cream cheese
- 1 15-oz. can corn
- 1 15-oz. can black beans (drained & rinsed)
- 2 green onions, sliced

- 1 C. sour cream
- ½ C. barbecue sauce
- 1 tsp. garlic powder
- 6 oz. chicken breast, grilled
- ½ C. Pepper Jack, shredded
- ½ C. cheddar, shredded

- 1 red onion, chopped
- 1 avocado, diced
- Barbecue sauce
- Tortilla chips

Preheat the grill on medium-low heat. Cut the blocks of cream cheese in half horizontally and set the pieces side by side in a greased 12-inch cast iron skillet. Dump the corn and black beans and sliced green onions on the cream cheese. Mix the sour cream, BBQ sauce, garlic powder, grilled chicken breast, and shredded Pepper Jack and cheddar cheeses; dump over the veggies in the pan and top with a little more cheese. Set the skillet on the grill, close the lid, and heat 10 to 15 minutes or until the cheese melts and everything is warm. Toss on some chopped red onion and diced avocado and add a drizzle of BBQ sauce. Serve warm with tortilla chips.

BUFFALO CHICKEN WITH BLUE CHEESE SLAW

MAKES 6 SERVINGS

- 1 C. packed coleslaw mix
- 1 finely chopped Granny Smith apple
- 2 finely chopped celery ribs
- 3 T. crumbled Gorgonzola cheese
- ¼ C. chopped fresh parsley
- 1 finely chopped green onion
- 3 T. olive oil
- 1½ T. apple cider vinegar
- ½ tsp. sugar

- Salt & black pepper to taste
- 1 C. wing sauce
- ½ C. unsalted butter, melted
- ⅓ C. ketchup
- 6 boneless, skinless chicken breast halves
- Softened butter
- 6 hefty buns, split (such as pretzel rolls)
- Ranch dressing

For the slaw, combine coleslaw mix, apple, celery, cheese, parsley, and green onion. Stir together oil, vinegar, sugar, salt, and black pepper; add to the slaw, stir to blend, and chill until serving time. In a big zippered plastic bag, mix the wing sauce, melted butter, and ketchup; remove ½ cup and set aside. Add the chicken to the bag and toss to coat. Marinate at least 30 minutes. Grease the grill grate and preheat the grill on medium heat. Toss the chicken on the grill (discard the marinade left in the bag) and cook until the internal temperature reaches 165°F, turning to brown both sides. Spread softened butter on the cut sides of the buns and grill until lightly toasted. Set the chicken on the buns; drizzle with ranch dressing and load on the slaw.

3 Beef

I love the culture of grilling. It creates an atmosphere that is festive but casual.
—*Bobby Flay*

BEEF
COOKING TIPS

To ensure safety and quality, grilled beef must be cooked to the minimum internal temperatures listed below. Larger cuts, like roasts, benefit from 15 minutes of standing time before carving. Since color is not a reliable indicator of doneness in beef, it is best to use a meat thermometer to measure internal temperature.

Cuts	Cook to this internal temperature
Beef steaks and beef roasts:	145° to 170°F
rare/medium rare:	145°F
medium:	160°F
well-done:	170°F
Ground beef:	160°F

Tender cuts of beef can be cooked by direct or indirect heat. Less tender cuts of meat require tenderizing and should be cooked with indirect heat for best results. Tenderizing can be done by pounding with a meat mallet, scoring with a sharp knife or marinating in a mixture containing an acidic ingredient like lemon juice, vinegar or wine. Meat should always be refrigerated during marinating.

GRILLED SIRLOIN STEAK

MAKES 4 SERVINGS

- 2 (12 to 14 oz.) beef top sirloin steaks*
- Salt and black pepper to taste
- Seasoned salt or garlic salt, optional

Sprinkle steaks with salt, black pepper and other seasonings to taste. Lightly oil the grate and preheat grill to medium-high heat. Place steaks on grate over direct heat and grill for 14 to 22 minutes (if 1 inch thick), turning once halfway through cooking time. Adjust time for steak's thickness and the degree of doneness desired. To serve, cut each steak in half and top with a favorite sauce.

Other tender beef steaks may be substituted such as or T-bone, porterhouse, ribeye, flat iron or tenderloin. Tenderloin steaks (also called filet mignon) are often wrapped with bacon to add flavor since they have very little fat of their own to flavor the meat.

LIME-MARINATED STEAK

MAKES 4 SERVINGS

- ¼ C. vegetable oil
- 6 dried chili peppers cut into strips
- 1 C. coarsely chopped onion
- 1½ tsp. minced fresh garlic
- ½ C. beef broth
- 2 T. fresh lime juice
- 2 tsp. cumin seed
- 1½ tsp. salt
- 1 tsp. brown sugar
- 4 New York steaks, tenderized
- Juice from 2 limes

In a medium skilled over medium-low heat, combine vegetable oil, chili pepper strips, chopped onion, and minced garlic; saute until onion is tender. Pour onion mixture in a blender and add beef broth, lime juice, cumin seed, salt, and brown sugar. Process until blended. Place tenderized steaks in a large sealable bag, pour half of the marinade over the steaks, and seal the bag. Place remaining marinade in an airtight container. Place bag with steaks and container with remaining marinade in refrigerator or cooler until ready to prepare. Preheat grill to medium heat. Place steaks over grill and baste with reserved marinade. Grill to taste. Before serving, brush with additional marinade and generously squeeze lime juice over cooked steaks.

MONTREAL GRILLED T-BONE

MAKES 4 SERVINGS

- 4 14-oz. T-bone steaks
- ½ C. beef stock
- ½ diced onion
- ½ tsp. chili flakes
- ½ C. chicken broth
- 2 oz. bourbon
- 1 oz. port
- ¼ tsp. Cajun seasoning
- Salt and pepper to taste

Combine first six ingredients in medium saucepan. Bring to a boil. Simmer uncovered for 4 minutes.

Sprinkle steaks with Cajun seasoning, salt, and pepper. Cook steaks on high heat until desired doneness. Place steaks on plate. Serve with sauce.

PORTERHOUSE WITH SPICY PARMESAN BUTTER

MAKES 2 SERVINGS

- 1 Porterhouse steak, approximately 3" thick
- ¼ C. olive oil
- 8 garlic cloves, minced
- 1 T. chopped fresh thyme
- 1 T. salt
- 2 tsp. ground black pepper
- 1½ tsp. chopped fresh rosemary

SPICY PARMESAN BUTTER

- 3 T. butter, room temperature
- 2 tsp. grated Parmesan cheese
- 1 anchovy fillet, drained and minced
- 1 tsp. paprika
- ½ tsp. Dijon mustard
- ½ tsp. Worcestershire sauce
- ¼ tsp. ground black pepper
- ¼ tsp. Tabasco sauce

Prepare butter by mixing all ingredients in a small bowl until blended. (Can be made 2 days ahead.) Refrigerate. When ready to use, remove from refrigerator and warm to room temperature.

Place steak in a glass dish. Whisk oil and next five ingredients in a small bowl to blend. Pour half of marinade over steak. Turn steak over, and coat with remaining marinade. Cover and refrigerate at least 2 hours and up to 24 hours, turning steak occasionally.

Preheat grill to medium. Remove meat from marinade, and grill to desired doneness or until internal temperature reaches 115°F to 130°F for medium-rare, approximately 18 minutes per side. Transfer steak to a platter; cover; and let rest for 5 minutes.

Cutting away from bone, slice each meat section into ⅓-inch slices. Spread Spicy Parmesan Butter over each portion, and serve.

SMOKY GRILLED MEAT LOAF

MAKES 8 TO 10 SERVINGS

- 1 lb. ground pork
- 1 lb. ground beef
- 1 lb. ground turkey
- 1 lb. center-cut bacon
- ¼ C. carrots, chopped
- ¼ C. celery, chopped
- ¼ C. white onion, chopped
- 3 large eggs, lightly beaten
- ¼ C. fine bread crumbs
- 5 large cloves garlic, roughly chopped
- ½ tsp. ground cumin
- ½ tsp. mustard powder
- ½ tsp. Worcestershire sauce
- ½ tsp. balsamic vinegar
- ¼ C. ketchup
- Salt and pepper to taste

In a skillet, cook bacon until it starts to brown. Remove bacon, but reserve fat in the skillet.

Add carrots, celery, and onion and a pinch of salt to the bacon fat. Cover, and cook until the vegetables are softened and slightly browned, about 3 to 5 minutes. Remove from heat, and let vegetables cool.

In a large bowl, thoroughly mix the meat with the eggs, cooked vegetables, and all remaining ingredients except for the bacon. Place the meat mixture into a metal-loaf pan, and weave bacon strips on top.

Preheat grill to high for about 10 minutes with hood closed. Turn center burner off, and reduce heat on outer burners. Temperature of cooking chamber with hood closed should remain steady at 350ºF.

Put soaked wood chips in a smoker box or foil on the grill. Place meat loaf in center, and close the hood. After about 30 minutes, check temperature inside grill. Add more wood chips if desired.

You can remove meat loaf from grill when a thermometer inserted in the center registers 160ºF. Cover with foil, and let rest at room temperature for 15 to 20 minutes before serving.

BASIC GRILLED SHISH KEBABS

MAKES 4 SERVINGS

- ½ C. sweet and tangy steak sauce (such as Heinz 57)
- ¼ C. lime juice
- 1½ lbs. boneless beef sirloin steak, cut into 1" cubes
- Salt and black pepper to taste
- Vegetables of choice: bell peppers, onions, potatoes, cherry tomatoes, mushrooms, pineapples, or other

Choice of fresh vegetables: red, green or yellow sweet bell peppers, cut in chunks; onions, cut in chunks; new potatoes, cut in half and parboiled for 10 to 12 minutes or until almost tender; cherry tomatoes; mushrooms; pineapple chunks.

In a small bowl, combine steak sauce and lime juice; mix well. Pour ½ cup of mixture into a large resealable plastic bag and add beef cubes. Seal bag and refrigerate to marinate meat for 1 hour, turning several times. Cover remaining marinade and refrigerate for basting later.

To cook, lightly oil the grate and preheat grill to medium heat. Remove meat from bag and discard marinade. On metal or soaked wooden skewers, alternately thread meat, potatoes and other vegetables as desired*. Sprinkle with salt and black pepper. Place kebabs on the grate and cook for 9 to 15 minutes or to desired doneness, turning often. Brush kebabs lightly with reserved sauce mixture during the last few minutes of cooking time.

If preferred, make separate skewers of meat and similar vegetables to assure even grilling. Grill onion and bell pepper kebabs for 10 minutes; grill tomato and mushroom kebabs for 7 minutes.

TAILGATE TIPS

MAKES 10 SERVINGS

- › 9 lbs. sirloin tips or rib-eye cubes
- › French rolls
- › American cheese
- › Vidalia onion, grilled

SAUCE
- › 1 C. ketchup
- › ⅛ T. molasses
- › ⅓ tsp. spicy brown or Dijon mustard

- › ⅛ tsp. soy sauce
- › ⅓ tsp. garlic powder
- › ⅓ tsp. hot pepper sauce
- › 1 tsp. black pepper

Trim any excess fat (keeping in mind the meat needs some fat to remain juicy throughout the grilling process), and cut meat into 2-inch cubes. Place tips in a large plastic container or bag.

In a large mixing bowl, combine sauce ingredients. Set aside some sauce for basting if you desire, and pour the rest of the sauce over tips. Mix well so that meat is completely coated. Refrigerate for 24 to 30 hours.

Preheat grill to medium-high heat. Grill tips to your desired doneness. Serve on rolls with cheese and onions. Note: To avoid a messy grill, coat your tips well the day before so that there's no need to slather on extra sauce.

INDIVIDUAL STEAK PIZZAS

MAKES 8 SERVINGS

- 1 lb. boneless beef sirloin steak
- 2 tsp. steak seasoning, divided
- 1 onion
- 1 green, red or yellow bell pepper
- 1 T. plus 1 tsp. olive oil, divided

- 1 (13.8 oz.) tube refrigerated pizza dough
- 1 C. prepared pizza sauce
- 2 C. shredded mozzarella or Monterey Jack cheese, divided
- 8 oz. crumbled blue cheese, optional

Lightly oil the grate and preheat grill to medium heat. Sprinkle both sides of steak with seasoning. Place steak on the grate and cook for 5 to 7 minutes on one side. Meanwhile, cut the onion and bell pepper into thick slices and brush with 1 teaspoon oil. Arrange vegetables on the grate to cook. Turn steaks and cook for 5 to 7 minutes longer or to desired doneness while vegetables continue to cook until tender-crisp. Remove steak and vegetables from the grill and cut into bite-size pieces; set aside.

Unroll dough and cut into four equal pieces. On a floured board, pat out each piece to larger rectangles about ¼ inch thick; brush top of each piece with remaining tablespoon oil. Place dough on the grate, oiled side down. Close lid and cook for 1 to 2 minutes or until grill marks show on crusts. Use tongs or a large spatula to carefully flip each crust over on the grate, moving it to indirect heat. Spread a portion of the sauce on each crust. Sprinkle about half of the mozzarella cheese over the four pizzas. Top each pizza with grilled steak, vegetables and optional blue cheese. Sprinkle remaining mozzarella cheese on top.

Close grill lid and cook pizzas for 3 to 4 minutes longer or until cheese is melted and crust is browned. Check pizzas often and rotate as needed for even baking. Slide pizzas onto a clean baking sheet before serving.

GRILLED ITALIAN BEEF ROAST

MAKES 12 TO 14 SERVINGS

> 1 (3 to 4 lb.) boneless beef sirloin tip roast
> 1 to 2 T. olive oil

> 1 (0.7 oz.) env. Italian dressing mix

Place grate 4 to 5 inches above heat. Lightly oil the grate and preheat grill for high heat for first part of grilling. Brush roast with oil and sprinkle dry Italian dressing evenly over meat; let stand at room temperature for about 15 minutes. Place roast on grate over direct heat and sear each side for 5 to 8 minutes or until well browned. Reduce heat and set up burners or charcoal for indirect grilling. Move the roast to the unheated part of grill for indirect heat. Cover grill and cook at about 300°F for 1½ hours without opening lid. Then open lid and insert a grill-safe meat thermometer into the thickest part of the meat. Cover and continue to cook the roast until thermometer reaches 145° to 150°F. Allow 30 to 90 minutes of additional time to cook roast to desired doneness. Remove roast from the grill and place it on a carving surface. Cover meat with foil and let stand 15 minutes to allow the internal temperature to rise about 5°. This will make the roast juicier and easier to carve.

SLOW-COOKED BEEF SHORT RIBS

MAKES 5 SERVINGS

> 10 beef short ribs (each approximately 3" long)
> Salt and black pepper to taste
> Olive oil
> 1 qt. beef broth (or water)

> 1 onion, coarsely chopped
> 1 (1 oz.) env. dry onion soup mix
> 2 C. sliced fresh mushrooms, optional
> 4 medium potatoes, peeled and cut into bite-size chunks

Preheat grill to high heat. Rinse ribs and pat dry. Peel off membrane on the back side of ribs. Sprinkle salt and black pepper generously over ribs and drizzle with oil. Place ribs on grate directly over heat and sear all sides for 1 to 2 minutes. When browned, transfer ribs to a grill-safe 9 x 13-inch pan placed over indirect heat. Pour broth over the ribs in pan. Arrange chopped onions on top and sprinkle dry soup mix over the ribs. Spread sliced mushrooms and potato chunks on top. Cover the grill and cook ribs in the pan over indirect heat (approximately 225°F) for 4 to 5 hours, basting the ribs with pan juices every 30 to 45 minutes.

Ribs are done when cooked through and very tender. Baste ribs one last time before moving them to a serving plate.* Serve with the potatoes and some of the juice, mushrooms and onions over the top.

* Ribs may be finished on the grate over direct heat for a few minutes before serving, if desired. See page 12 for additional information about direct and indirect heat.

CHEESE-STUFFED MEATBALL KEBABS

MAKES 4 TO 6 SERVINGS

- 1 egg, lightly beaten
- ⅓ C. grated Parmesan cheese
- 2 cloves garlic, minced
- ½ tsp. salt
- ⅛ tsp. black pepper
- 1 tsp. dried Italian seasoning
- 1½ lbs. lean ground beef

- 2 oz. fontina or mozzarella cheese, cubed
- 8 canned artichoke hearts, drained
- 1 (6 to 8 oz.) pkg. fresh cremini mushrooms
- 1 pt. grape tomatoes
- Warm Balsamic Glaze*
- Hot cooked rice

In a large bowl, combine egg, Parmesan cheese, garlic, salt, black pepper and Italian seasoning. Add ground beef and mix well, using hands as needed. Divide meatball mixture into approximately 16 portions. Shape each portion around one cheese cube to make meatballs. Thread meatballs, artichokes, mushrooms and tomatoes alternately on 16 (10-inch) metal or soaked wooden skewers, leaving a small space between items.

To cook, lightly oil the grate and preheat grill to medium heat. Place kebabs on the grate and grill for 5 to 6 minutes or until meat is partially cooked. Transfer half of the Warm Balsamic Glaze into a small bowl for brushing. Turn kebabs and brush them with half of the glaze, continuing to grill for an additional 5 to 6 minutes or until meat is cooked through and internal temperature reaches 160°F. Serve kebabs over rice and drizzle with remaining warmed glaze.

Warm Balsamic Glaze:
In a small saucepan over medium heat, combine ⅓ cup balsamic vinegar, 2 teaspoons olive oil, ½ teaspoon minced garlic, ¼ teaspoon salt, ⅛ teaspoon black pepper and ¼ teaspoon Italian seasoning. Bring mixture to a boil while stirring; reduce heat and simmer uncovered for 4 minutes or until reduced to about ¼ cup.

THE AMERICAN BURGER

MAKES 4 SERVINGS

- 1½ lb. ground beef
- 1 tsp. Worcestershire sauce
- 2 T. fresh chopped parsley
- 2 tsp. onion powder
- 1 tsp. garlic powder
- 1 tsp. salt
- 1 tsp. pepper
- 4 hamburger buns, split
- Ketchup, mustard, chopped onions, relish, cheese, optional

Preheat grill to medium heat. In a medium bowl, combine ground beef, Worcestershire sauce, chopped parsley, onion powder, garlic powder, salt, and pepper. Mix lightly but thoroughly. Shape mixture into four burgers, each about ½ inch thick. Place burgers on hot grate. Cook burgers over grill 8 to 10 minutes, turning once, until cooked as desired. Remove burgers from grate and place on buns. Garnish burgers with ketchup, mustard, chopped onions, and relish as desired.

SMOKED DEEP-DISH BURGERS

- Wood chips for smoking
- 1 T. butter
- 1 (8 oz.) pkg. sliced white mushrooms
- 1 red bell pepper, diced
- ½ C. chopped sweet onion
- 2 T. steak sauce (use your fave)
- 4 thick-cut bacon strips, cooked crisp & crumbled

- 3½ lbs. ground beef
- 1 beer or soda can for forming patties
- 12 thick-cut bacon strips, optional
- Coarse salt & black pepper
- 12 slices of your favorite cheese (sharp cheddar & Pepper Jack used here)

DIY Smoker Pouch: Dump soaked wood chips onto a piece of heavy-duty foil. Fold over the edges of the foil several times to make a pouch, sealing the chips inside. Poke some holes in the top of the pouch and set it on the grill grate, directly over the burner on the hot side of the grill.

Soak a great big handful of wood chips in water for 30 minutes, then drain. In the meantime, melt the butter in a skillet and sauté the mushrooms, bell pepper, and onion until softened. Stir in the steak sauce and cooked bacon and set aside. Line a rimmed baking sheet with foil and spritz with cooking spray. Form the ground beef into six equal-sized balls and arrange them on the baking sheet. Clean the outside of the beer or soda can and coat it with cooking spray. Press the can firmly into a meatball to form a cup, pressing the edges of the meat to an even thickness and fixing any cracks; wrap each with two bacon strips, if you'd like, and secure with toothpicks. Remove the can and repeat with the remaining meatballs. Season with salt and black pepper and fill with the mushroom mixture.

Grease the grill grate and preheat the grill to 300°F for indirect cooking. For a charcoal grill, toss a big handful of soaked wood chips directly on hot coals. For a gas grill, place wood chips in a smoker box. Wait until the wood smokes for 10 minutes before grilling food. Set the stuffed burgers on the cool side of the grill. Close the grill lid and cook 30 to 45 minutes; top each burger with two cheese slices. Cover and cook 1 to 1½ hours longer until the internal temperature of the meat reaches 160°F, maintaining the grill temperature throughout. Do not flip the burgers.

GUACAMOLE BURGER

MAKES 6 SERVINGS

- ❭ 2 lbs. ground chuck
- ❭ 2 to 3 heads of garlic, roasted
- ❭ 2 C. mayonnaise
- ❭ ½ tsp. lemon juice
- ❭ 1 T. Worcestershire sauce
- ❭ 1 tsp. coarse salt

- ❭ ½ tsp. freshly ground black pepper
- ❭ 2 T. Tex-Mex Rub
- ❭ 6 thick slices ripe tomato
- ❭ 6 lettuce leaves
- ❭ 6 large hamburger buns
- ❭ Pre-made guacamole

TEX-MEX RUB
- ❭ 2 T. chili powder
- ❭ 4 tsp. garlic salt
- ❭ 2½ tsp. onion powder
- ❭ 2 tsp. ground cumin
- ❭ 1½ tsp. dried oregano
- ❭ ¾ tsp. cayenne pepper

Mix all ingredients for the Tex-Mex Rub in a small bowl. Set aside.

For garlic mayonnaise, squeeze one bulb roasted garlic from its skin into a medium bowl. Using fork, mash garlic, pressing against side of bowl. Add mayonnaise and lemon juice, and mix well. Refrigerate mixture until ready to serve burgers.

Place second bulb of roasted garlic in a large bowl, and mash with fork against side of bowl. Add ground chuck, Worcestershire sauce, salt, and pepper, and mix with hands until just combined. Gently form six patties approximately ½ to ¾ inches thick. Coat patties with dry rub.

Preheat grill to high. Grill burgers for approximately 1 minute on each side. Reduce grill temperature to medium, and continue cooking burgers for 4 to 5 minutes more per side. Toast buns at edge of grill. Spread garlic mayonnaise on one half of each bun, and top with lettuce, burger, guacamole, and tomato slice. Sprinkle with salt and pepper.

CAJUN BURGERS

- 2 lbs. ground beef
- 1 C. seasoned breadcrumbs
- 2 T. ground coriander
- 2 T. Cajun spice
- ¼ tsp. dried steak seasoning
- ¼ tsp. dried oregano
- 1 tsp. Worcestershire sauce
- ¼ tsp. garlic powder
- 2 jalapeño peppers, seeded and diced
- 6 to 8 hamburger buns, toasted

Combine all ingredients except the buns in a large mixing bowl with ground beef. Form into patties, 6–8 ounces each.

Cook on high heat until desired doneness, 6 to 8 minutes per side for medium.

GRILLED BEEF TACOS WITH AVOCADO SALSA

MAKES 6 SERVINGS

> 4 beef top-blade (flat-iron) steaks, about 8 oz. each
> 18 small corn tortillas (6" to 7" diameter)

MARINADE

> 1 C. prepared tomatillo salsa
> ⅓ C. chopped fresh cilantro
> 2 T. fresh lime juice
> 2 tsp. minced garlic
> ½ tsp. salt
> ¼ tsp. pepper

AVOCADO SALSA

> 1½ C. prepared tomatillo salsa
> 1 large avocado, diced
> ⅔ C. fresh cilantro, chopped
> ½ C. white onion, minced
> 1 T. fresh lime juice
> 1 tsp. garlic, minced
> ½ tsp. salt

TOPPINGS

> Minced white onion
> Chopped fresh cilantro
> Lime wedges

Combine marinade ingredients in a small bowl. Place steaks and marinade in a food-safe plastic bag; turn steaks to coat. Close bag securely, and marinate steaks in refrigerator for 15 minutes to 2 hours.

Remove steaks from marinade; discard marinade. Place steaks on grill over medium heat. Grill, covered, 10 to 14 minutes for medium rare to medium doneness, turning once.

Meanwhile, combine avocado salsa ingredients in a medium bowl. Set aside.

Place tortillas on grill. Grill until warm and slightly charred. Remove; keep warm. Slice steaks, and serve in grilled tortillas with avocado salsa. Top with onion, cilantro, and lime wedges as desired.

PRIME RIB ROAST

MAKES 8 TO 12 SERVINGS

BEEF RUB
- › 1 T. kosher salt
- › 1 T. coarse ground black pepper
- › 1 tsp. dried minced onion
- › 1 tsp. dried minced garlic
- › ½ tsp. dried parsley
- › ½ tsp. red pepper flakes

ROAST
- › 4–6 lb. bone-in beef rib roast
- › 1–2 T. vegetable oil
- › 1 qt. beef stock
- › 1 oz. dried porcini mushrooms

Mix together the salt, pepper, onion, garlic, parsley, and pepper flakes. Remove the butcher's twine and lightly coat the roast and ribs with oil. Season on all sides (including the space between the ribs and roast) with the dry rub. Re-tie the beef roast and ribs back together. Let sit at room temperature for an hour.

Set up your grill for indirect heat and preheat to low (250°F–300°F). Place the roast, bone-side down, on a roasting rack and pan combination. Add enough stock to fill the pan about 1 inch deep. Add the dried mushrooms. Place the roast and pan on the grill on the indirect side where you don't have any burners on. Close the grill lid and cook until the rib roast hits 10°F less than your desired level of doneness. This should take about 3 hours for medium rare. It's a good idea to turn the roast around every 45 minutes or so. (For rare, pull at internal temperature of 115°F. For medium rare, 125°F. For medium, 135°F.)

Remove the roast and pan set up and let rest at room temperature until the internal temperature stops rising—about 20 minutes. Meanwhile, turn up the grill heat to high (500°F). Taste the au jus (seasoned broth in the pan) and season with salt and pepper to taste. Keep warm. Fully remove the rib bones. Place the rib bones cut side down over the heat. Sear the roast 2–3 minutes on the cut side and 1–2 minutes on the other sides. Remove from the grill. You can let it rest for 5 minutes but it isn't needed—it already settled during the previous rest. Slice, top with some of the porcini au jus, and serve.

4 Pork

Grilling is an easy tradition to start at any age!
To get started, one only needs a modest investment
in equipment and a little bit of outdoor space.
—Barton Seaver

PORK
COOKING TIPS

Fully cooked pork should reach an internal temperature of 160°F before eating to ensure safety. When cooked correctly, the meat should be juicy and tender. Color is not an indication of doneness, so the meat may retain a slightly pink color in the center. To shred pork roasts, it is often desirable to cook the meat until it reaches a higher internal temperature for added tenderness.

Pork chops (½" to 1½" thick):	145°F
Tenderloins:	145°F
Pork roast:	145° to 190°F
Ground pork:	160°F
Ham:	145°F
Reheating fully cooked ham:	145°F
Fully cooked smoked pork chops:	145°F

GRILLED PORK CHOPS

> 1 tsp. ground cumin
> 1 tsp. mild chili powder
> Salt and black pepper to taste

> 1 T. olive oil
> 4 pork loin or rib chops, ¾" to 1" thick

Lightly oil the grate and preheat grill to medium heat*. In a small bowl, combine cumin, chili powder, salt and black pepper; mix well. Brush both sides of each pork chop with oil. Sprinkle with cumin mixture.

To cook, place chops on the grate and grill for 8 to 14 minutes, turning once. Adjust cooking time for thickness of meat; chops are done when browned on both sides and internal temperature reaches 145°F.

If grilling thinner pork chops, use medium-high heat and shorten grilling time to approximately 4 minutes per side. Boneless pork chops may also be used. If you purchase thick boneless chops (1½ inches), try wrapping two strips of bacon around the outside edge of each chop and securing with toothpicks before marinating or grilling.

SPIT-ROASTED PORK CHOPS

MAKES 6 SERVINGS

> 2 T. olive oil
> 8 center-cut pork chops, ¾" thick

BBQ RUB
> ¼ C. kosher salt
> ¼ C. paprika
> ½ tsp. cayenne pepper
> ⅓ C. brown sugar
> 1 T. garlic powder
> 2 tsp. celery salt

GLAZE
> ¼ C. fresh lime juice
> ½ C. honey
> 2 tsp. dried thyme
> Pinch of cayenne
> ⅛ tsp. ground cumin
> ¼ C. fresh cilantro leaves, chopped
> 2 limes, each cut into 8 wedges

Pour olive oil into shallow dish, and mix with barbecue rub ingredients. Dip chops into spice mixture, turning to coat evenly. Preheat grill to medium-high. Coat rotisserie basket with nonstick cooking spray; lay chops in basket; and close lid tightly. Load basket onto spit rod.

Combine glaze ingredients. When chops have cooked for 10 minutes, stop rotisserie and baste chops with glaze. Restart rotisserie, and continue to grill chops another 25 minutes or until thickest part reaches 160°F, stopping rotisserie three more times to baste. Remove chops from basket; garnish with cilantro and lime wedges. Serve.

AUTUMN PORK CHOP STACKS

MAKES 4 SERVINGS

- 4 (¾" to 1" thick) pork chops*
- 4 thick apple slices, unpeeled
- 4 thick sweet potato slices, peeled
- 4 thick red onion slices

- ½ tsp. dried savory
- ⅛ tsp. ground nutmeg
- Salt and black pepper to taste
- 4 tsp. butter

In a nonstick skillet over medium-hot heat, lightly brown pork chops on both sides. Cut four (12-inch) pieces of heavy-duty aluminum foil and spray the dull side of each piece with nonstick cooking spray. Place a pork chop in the center of each piece. Top each chop with one apple slice, one sweet potato slice and one red onion slice. Sprinkle some savory, nutmeg, salt and black pepper on each stack. Top each with a teaspoon of butter. Wrap the foil around the stacked foods, sealing edges well and allowing extra room for air to circulate.

To cook, preheat grill to medium heat. Place foil packs over coals and cook for 40 to 50 minutes or until meat is cooked through and vegetables are tender. Turn packs several times while grilling. Remove from grill and let packs rest for 5 minutes before carefully cutting open to eat.

Shorten cooking time if using thin pork chops (½ to ¾ inch thick).

> Make **BBQ Pork Foil Packs** with thin pork chops, 2" pieces of sweet corn on the ear, wedges of new potatoes and baby carrots sliced lengthwise. Omit the seasonings listed above, but mix together ½ cup bottled barbeque sauce, ¼ cup honey and 2 teaspoons ground cumin. Season with salt and pepper. Spoon 3 tablespoons of sauce over each serving, wrap in foil and grill packs over medium heat for 20 minutes, or until pork is almost cooked through, turning once. Remove from grill and let packs rest 5 minutes before cutting open to eat.

PERFECT GRILLED PORK TENDERLOIN

MAKES 6 TO 8 SERVINGS

> 1 tsp. garlic powder
> 1 tsp. salt
> ¾ to 1 tsp. black pepper

> 2 (1 lb.) pork tenderloins
> 1 T. olive oil
> 1 C. bottled barbeque sauce, optional

In a small bowl, combine garlic powder, salt and black pepper; mix well. Sprinkle over all sides of pork and pat gently into meat. Brush meat lightly with oil and let stand while heating the grill.

To cook, lightly oil the grate and preheat grill to medium-high heat. Place tenderloins on the grate over heat and sear for 1 to 2 minutes on each side until browned. Reduce temperature and arrange to continue grilling with indirect heat. Move pork to cooler side of grill, close lid and cook for 25 to 30 minutes. Turn meat over, brush with barbeque sauce, if desired, and cook for 8 to 10 minutes longer, or until internal temperature nearly reaches 145°F. Remove from grill and let stand under a foil tent for 5 minutes before slicing.

To prevent the narrow tenderloin ends from drying out on the grill, trim off the ends before grilling and slice them into smaller chunks. Grill the large pieces of tenderloin as directed above, but thread the chunks onto double skewers and grill them separately for a shorter period of time. If desired, slice thinly for use in fajitas.

Apple wood chips add a great smoked flavor to grilled pork tenderloin.

HAWAIIAN HAM

- Juice reserved from 1 8.25-oz. can sliced pineapple
- 1 to 2 T. soy sauce
- 1 tsp. ground ginger

- 1 clove garlic, minced
- Fully cooked ham, sliced into 4 steaks (1" thick)
- Canned pineapple slices

Blend together pineapple juice, soy sauce, ginger, and garlic. Score ham in diamond pattern. Put steaks into a plastic storage bag, and add liquid. Marinate at least 30 minutes. Remove ham, and reserve marinade. Preheat grill to high. Grill ham until heated through, brushing often with marinade. After about 3 minutes on one side, turn steaks, and put pineapple slices directly on grill or in grill basket. Place pineapple slices on top of ham slices before serving.

SMOKED PULLED PORK SANDWICHES

MAKES 12 SERVINGS

- 1 (5 to 6 lb.) pork shoulder roast or pork butt
- 3 T. vegetable oil
- 2 T. salt
- 1 T. black pepper
- 2 T. paprika
- 1 tsp. cayenne pepper, optional
- 1 C. apple juice, optional
- 12 large sandwich buns or kaiser rolls, split
- Sauce of choice

Trim excess fat, rinse meat and pat dry. Coat meat with oil. In a small bowl, combine salt, black pepper, paprika and optional cayenne pepper; mix well. Sprinkle pork with salt mixture and gently rub over meat. Cover meat in plastic wrap and refrigerate for 8 to 24 hours before grilling.

To cook, lightly oil the grate, preheat grill to medium-low heat (225° to 250°F) and arrange for indirect cooking. Add a pouch of hickory chips to produce smoke. Place meat on the grate over cooler side of the grill and close lid. For the first 2 hours of grilling, check the heat every 30 minutes and add briquettes or adjust temperature to maintain heat and smoke. After 2 hours, transfer meat to a roasting rack inside a heavy-duty foil roasting pan and add 1 cup water (or apple juice). Cover pan tightly with foil. Increase grill temperature to 350°F and cook for 2 to 3 hours or until internal temperature reaches 190°F. Rotate pan occasionally. When a fork inserted into the meat turns easily, the meat is ready. Turn off heat and allow meat to rest for 20 to 30 minutes. Shred or slice the pork. Serve meat on buns with sauce or place shredded pork into the sauce and heat well before serving on buns.

BEER-BASTED BABY BACK RIBS

MAKES 4 TO 6 SERVINGS

- 8 lbs. baby back pork ribs, cut into 4-rib sections
- 6 C. beer
- 2½ C. brown sugar
- 1½ C. apple cider vinegar
- 1½ T. chili powder
- 1½ T. ground cumin
- 1 T. dry mustard
- 2 tsp. salt
- 2 tsp. dried crushed red pepper
- 2 bay leaves

Bring first nine ingredients to a boil in a large pot. Reduce heat, and simmer about 1 minute to blend flavors. Add half of ribs to sauce. Cover pot, and simmer until ribs are tender, turning frequently, about 25 minutes. Transfer ribs to baking dish. Repeat with remaining ribs. Boil barbecue sauce until reduced to 3 cups, about 40 minutes. Discard bay leaves. (Can be prepared 1 day ahead. Cover ribs and sauce separately, and refrigerate. Warm sauce before continuing.)

Preheat grill to medium, and oil the grill grates. Brush ribs with some of sauce; sprinkle with salt. Grill ribs until heated through, browned, and well-glazed, brushing occasionally with sauce, about 6 minutes per side.

COLA RIBS

MAKES 6 SERVINGS

- 2 racks baby back ribs, approx. 3 lbs. each
- 3 sweet potatoes
- 3 ears corn
- Canola oil

MARINADE
- 2 C. cola
- ½ C. bourbon
- ½ C. brown sugar
- 2 T. mustard powder
- 2 T. chili flakes

- 1 T. garlic, minced
- 3 sprigs fresh rosemary
- ½ bag char wood (⅔ soaked in cool water for 2 hours or until saturated)

Place ribs in nonreactive glass dish. Mix marinade ingredients in medium-size bowl. Pour marinade over ribs, and cover with plastic wrap. Allow ribs to marinate for 4 hours.

Preheat grill to medium heat for indirect cooking. Add two-thirds of drained soaked wood and remaining dry char wood to smoking tray. Mix, and allow wood to smoke. Once smoke is achieved, reduce heat to low, and add more wet chips.

Place ribs over the side of the grill that does not have direct heat. Close lid, and smoke for 3 hours or until ribs are falling off the bone. While cooking, continue to add wet chips to the tray. Remove ribs from grill, and loosely tent them with foil. Let ribs rest for 10 minutes before serving.

Spray potatoes with canola oil. Sear potatoes 3 minutes on each side. Move to tray over indirect heat, and cook for 20 minutes or until tender; grill corn over direct heat, turning often, for about 5 minutes.

SUMMERTIME BBQ RIBS

MAKES 6 SERVINGS

- ¼ C. brown sugar
- 2 tsp. seasoned salt
- 2 tsp. chili powder
- 4 lbs. pork back ribs
- ¼ C. prepared yellow mustard
- 4 C. hickory or fruitwood chunks
- ¼ C. bottled barbeque sauce
- Additional barbeque sauce

In a small bowl, combine brown sugar, seasoned salt and chili powder; set aside. Rinse ribs and remove membrane. If desired, cut ribs into serving pieces. Brush ribs with mustard and sprinkle with brown sugar mixture. Cover and refrigerate for 6 to 24 hours.

One hour before grilling, soak wood chunks in water. Remove the grate and lightly oil it. Preheat grill to medium heat. Place a drip pan holding 1 inch of water in the center and arrange hot coals around pan. Sprinkle damp wood over the coals before replacing grate. Place ribs, meaty side up, on the grate over the drip pan, but not over the coals. Cover the grill and cook ribs over indirect heat for 1¼ to 1½ hours or until tender. Add more coals and wood as needed. Brush ribs with ¼ cup barbeque sauce and grill for 5 minutes longer. Serve with additional barbeque sauce as desired. (If using very low heat on the charcoal grill, cook ribs for up to 3 hours.)

GRILLED BRATS

MAKES 5 SERVINGS

- 1¼ lbs. bratwurst sausages
- 2 12-oz. light beers, room temperature
- 1 large sweet onion, sliced into wedges
- 2–3 T. butter
- 1 tsp. roasted garlic paste or 2 cloves minced
- ½ tsp. coarse ground black pepper
- Salt to taste
- 5 hard rolls or hot dog buns
- Toppings of your choice

Preheat grill to 300°F–350°F. Place the onions, butter, roasted garlic (or minced garlic), beer, black pepper, and a few pinches of salt to taste in the steam pan.

Place the brats on the grill and grill for 20 minutes, flipping and shifting them around every five minutes.

Place the steam pan on the grill and place the brats in the steam pan, close the grill lid and cook for 20 minutes. Note: It should start simmering after 5 or so minutes, but not a full boil. If it starts to simmer too rapidly, reduce the heat. Remove pan from the grill. Serve with buns and choice of toppings.

ITALIAN SAUSAGE & PEPPERS

MAKES 4 SERVINGS

- ½ C. olive oil
- ¼ C. red wine vinegar
- 2 T. fresh chopped parsley
- 1 T. dried oregano
- 2 cloves garlic, crushed
- 1 tsp. salt
- 1 tsp. pepper
- 4 hot or sweet Italian sausage links
- 1 large onion, peeled and sliced into rings
- 1 large red bell pepper, quartered
- Large buns, optional

In a small bowl, combine olive oil, vinegar, chopped parsley, dried oregano, crushed garlic, salt, and pepper. Place sausages, sliced onion, and quartered red bell pepper in a large sealable bag and pour marinade over ingredients in bag. Seal bag and place in refrigerator or cooler until ready to prepare. Preheat grill to medium heat. Place a heavy skillet over heated grill. Empty contents of bag into skillet and heat, covered, about 4 to 5 minutes. Continue to grill until sausages are cooked through. To serve, spoon cooked sausages and some of the onions and peppers onto each serving plate or in large buns.

GRILLED PEANUTTY-PORK BURGERS

MAKES 4 SERVINGS

- ½ C. finely chopped onion
- ¼ C. finely chopped dry roasted peanuts
- 1 T. snipped fresh cilantro
- 1 T. grated fresh gingerroot
- 4 cloves garlic, minced, divided
- ¼ tsp. crushed red pepper flakes
- 1 tsp. salt
- 1 lb. lean ground pork
- 1 T. sesame oil
- ⅓ C. bottled chili sauce or Asian sweet chili sauce
- 1 T. creamy peanut butter
- 4 French rolls or hamburger buns, split
- 1 C. shredded bok choy
- Additional chopped peanuts, other toppings as desired

Lightly oil the grate and preheat grill to medium heat. In a medium bowl, combine onion, ¼ cup peanuts, cilantro, gingerroot, 3 cloves garlic, red pepper flakes and salt. Add ground pork and mix well, using hands as needed. Shape mixture into four ½-inch-thick patties. Brush patties with oil; cover and set aside. Place patties directly over heat and cook for 5 to 7 minutes. (If using a gas grill, cover grill during cooking.) Flip patties once and continue to cook for 5 to 6 minutes more or until meat is done and internal temperature reaches 160°F.

Meanwhile, in a small bowl, whisk together chili sauce, peanut butter and remaining 1 clove minced garlic; set aside. Before serving, toast rolls on grill. Place a portion of the bok choy on the bottom of each roll and top with a grilled patty, some sauce mixture, additional chopped peanuts and bun top.

ROLL OVER BIG DOGS

- Olive oil
- 3 poblano peppers
- 2 to 3 T. of your favorite mustard
- 1 to 2 T. chopped onion
- 1 to 2 T. salsa
- Black pepper to taste

- 1 (16 oz.) can refried beans (any variety)
- 16 (8") flour tortillas
- 1 (16 oz.) pkg. shredded Colby Jack cheese
- 8 (¼ lb.) hot dogs
- Cheese dip, sour cream & salsa

Grease the grill grate and preheat the grill on high heat. Drizzle oil over the peppers and set them on the hot grill, cooking until they're nicely charred, turning occasionally. Remove and discard the skin, leaving some of the char in place; coarsely chop the peppers, discarding seeds. Mix the mustard, onion, salsa, black pepper, and beans together and spread evenly over one side of each tortilla. Divide the cheese and chopped peppers over the beans on half the tortillas and stack those on top of the remaining ones, bean sides up; set aside.

Heat the hot dogs on the grill until they're cooked the way you like them. Remove them from the grill but don't turn off the heat. Place a grilled dog on each of the tortilla stacks and roll up to enclose that puppy tightly inside. Spritz the roll-ups with cooking spray and set them on the grill until they have nice grill marks all around, turning as needed. Set out cheese dip, sour cream, and salsa for dipping.

QUICK BACON-AVOCADO PIZZAS

MAKES 4 PIZZAS

- 4 artisan thin flatbread pizza crusts
- Olive oil
- ½ C. tomato sauce
- 1½ C. each shredded cheddar and provolone cheeses
- 6 bacon strips, cooked & chopped
- 1 or 2 Roma tomatoes, very thinly sliced
- Red onion, finely chopped
- 2 avocados, seeded, peeled & diced

Make sure all your toppings are ready and setting by the grill, then preheat the grill on low heat. Drizzle the crusts with oil and set them oil-side down on the grill for a couple of minutes, until grill marks appear. Flip them over onto a flat cookie sheet and spread each with about 2 tablespoons of the sauce. Divide half the cheese among the crusts. Top each with the bacon, tomato, onion, and avocado, and sprinkle the remaining cheese over all. Slide the pizzas onto the grill and cook several minutes, until the cheese is melted and grill marks appear on the bottom. Serve hot.

PORK BURGERS

MAKES 6 SERVINGS

- 2 lbs. ground pork
- 1 tsp. ground ginger
- ½ C. diced green onion
- ¼ tsp. ground allspice
- Salt and black pepper to taste
- BBQ sauce
- 6 pineapple rings
- Butter
- 6 hamburger buns
- Spinach leaves
- 6 slices deli ham

Dump ground pork, ginger, green onion, allspice, salt, and black pepper into a bowl and mix with your hands until just combined. Form six large patties and press an indentation in the middle of each. Grease the grill grates and preheat the grill on medium heat. Toss the patties on the grill and brush with BBQ sauce; cook with the lid closed until brown on the bottom, then flip and brush with more sauce. Cook until done (160°F), then set aside for 5 minutes.

In the meantime, toss the pineapple slices on the grate and heat until lightly browned, turning once. Butter the cut sides of the buns and set them butter side down until nicely toasted. Build your burgers with spinach, more BBQ sauce, a slice of ham, and a grilled pineapple slice, all sandwiched between the grilled buns.

5 Seafood

I love grilling. Grilling is an incredible way to keep healthy.
—*Curtis Stone*

SEAFOOD
COOKING TIPS

Some fish are fragile and don't cook well on a grill; avoid very thin, flat fish, such as sole or flounder. Cooking time for seafood will depend upon the thickness of each piece, but like other foods, seafood continues to cook after being removed from the heat. To avoid overcooking, take fish off the grate when the center begins to turn opaque and the thickest part starts to flake when pressed with a fork.

Brush both the seafood and grate lightly with canola oil to prevent sticking. A seafood basket makes grilling any type of seafood easy. Leaving the skin on fresh fish will help it stay together during grilling; remove it just before serving, if desired. Whereas tongs work well for turning beef or pork, spatulas work better for most seafood. Fish steaks are crosswise cuts, about 1" thick, through the fish's backbone. Fillets come from the sides of the fish and generally have the skin and bones removed. Fillets can be purchased as an entire half of the fish or cut into single serving pieces.

Most Fish:	145°F

CEDAR PLANK SALMON

MAKES 6 SERVINGS

- 3 (12") untreated cedar planks
- ⅓ C. vegetable oil
- 1 tsp. sesame oil
- 1½ T. rice vinegar
- ⅓ C. soy sauce
- ¼ C. chopped green onions
- 1 T. grated fresh gingerroot
- 1 tsp. minced garlic
- 2 (2 lb.) salmon fillets, skin removed (about 1" thick)

Soak cedar planks in warm water for 4 to 24 hours. In a shallow glass baking dish, combine vegetable oil, sesame oil, vinegar, soy sauce, onions, gingerroot and garlic; mix well. Place salmon in the marinade and turn to coat well. Cover and refrigerate to marinate for 15 to 60 minutes.

To cook, lightly oil the grate and preheat grill to medium heat. Place wet planks on the grate; boards are heated and ready for cooking when they start to smoke and make a crackling sound. Lightly brush the planks with oil using a paper towel and tongs. Place salmon fillets on the planks and discard marinade. Cover grill and cook for about 20 minutes or until fish flakes easily with a fork.

You may reuse planks if they are not too charred; just wash with warm water and let air dry.

FAST & SPICY HALIBUT

MAKES 4 SERVINGS

> 4 halibut steaks or fillets (4 to 6 oz. each), fresh, thawed, or frozen
> 1 T. paprika
> 1½ tsp. each dried oregano and dried thyme
> 1 tsp. each onion powder and garlic powder
> 1 tsp. each black pepper and salt
> ½ tsp. cayenne pepper, or to taste
> 1½ T. butter, melted

Preheat grill to medium high. Mix together all dry-seasoning ingredients until well combined. Rinse any ice glaze from frozen halibut under cold water; pat dry with paper towel. Place fish on a spray-coated or foil-lined baking sheet. Brush butter onto top surfaces of halibut, and sprinkle with ½ teaspoon seasoning mixture.

Grill halibut 5 to 7 inches from heat for 13 to 15 minutes for frozen halibut or 8 minutes for fresh fish. Note: For best results with frozen fish, cook halibut 4 minutes before adding butter and spices. Cook just until fish is opaque throughout.

HALIBUT & APPLE KEBABS

MAKES 4 SERVINGS

- 1½ lbs. halibut (or cod or red snapper)
- 1 red onion
- 1 yellow or red apple, cored
- 1 sweet red or green bell pepper, cored and seeded
- ½ C. unsweetened apple juice
- 2 T. lime juice
- 2 T. olive oil
- 2 T. finely diced onion
- ½ tsp. dried thyme
- 1 tsp. salt
- ¼ tsp. black pepper

Rinse halibut and pat dry. Cut the fish, red onion, apple and bell pepper into 1 inch pieces; set aside. In a small bowl, combine apple juice, lime juice, oil, diced onion, thyme, salt and black pepper; mix well. Divide the marinade mixture between two large resealable plastic bags. Add halibut pieces to one bag; seal and turn to coat fish. Add onion, apple and bell pepper to the second bag; seal and turn to coat pieces. Refrigerate bags to marinate fish and apple mixture for 4 to 6 hours, turning occasionally.

To cook, lightly oil the grate and preheat grill to medium heat. Remove fish and discard marinade. Remove fruit and vegetables and reserve that marinade for basting. On eight metal or soaked wooden skewers, alternately thread pieces of fish, onion, apple and bell pepper as desired. Place skewers on the grate over direct heat. Cook uncovered for 6 to 10 minutes, turning once, until fish flakes easily with a fork and fruit and vegetables are tender. Baste frequently during grilling with reserved marinade.

The apple juice mixture may also be used to marinate whole halibut steaks or pieces before grilling.

GRILLED SWORDFISH WITH CITRUS SALSA

MAKES 4 SERVINGS

- 4 5-oz. swordfish steaks
- 1 T. corn oil
- Salt and pepper to taste

CITRUS SALSA
- 1 ruby red grapefruit
- ½ orange, peeled
- ½ lime, peeled
- 1 lemon, peeled
- 1 medium red onion
- 1 C. diced red, green, and yellow bell pepper
- 1 T. chopped cilantro
- 1 T. chopped mint
- 1 oz. tequila

Prepare the citrus salsa—mix all ingredients except swordfish, corn oil, salt, and pepper, and let marinate for a couple of hours.

Season the swordfish steaks with salt and pepper to personal taste. Brush lightly with one tablespoon corn oil. Grill for about 5 minutes per side until fish is firm and slightly opaque. (Use a knife to check.)

Spoon the salsa over the charbroiled swordfish steaks. Garnish with mint sprigs. Great served with saffron rice, fresh asparagus, and baby carrots.

For the salsa: Section and remove white membrane from grapefruit, orange, lime, and lemon; then cut each fruit into bite-size pieces. Finely dice onion. Mix together fruit, onion, peppers, cilantro, mint, and tequila. Let salsa marinate for 1 to 2 hours before serving.

GRILLED TUNA SANDWICHES

MAKES 4 SERVINGS

- 2 T. soy sauce
- 1 T. sesame oil
- 1 T. orange juice
- ½ tsp. ground ginger
- 3 T. mayonnaise
- 4 (4 oz.) fresh tuna steaks (about ½" thick)
- 4 hamburger buns or kaiser rolls, split
- Lettuce leaves
- 1 large tomato, sliced
- Cucumber slices

In an 8-inch square baking dish, blend together soy sauce, oil, orange juice and ginger; remove 1 tablespoon of the mixture and stir it into the mayonnaise in a small bowl; cover and refrigerate for later use. Add tuna to remaining mixture in dish and turn to coat fish. Cover and refrigerate to marinate tuna at least 15 minutes or up to 2 hours.

To cook, lightly coat the grate with oil and preheat grill to medium heat. Remove tuna from dish and discard marinade. Place tuna on the grate over heat and grill for about 10 minutes or until fish flakes easily with a fork, turning once. To serve, spread reserved flavored mayonnaise on the cut sides of each bun; add lettuce, grilled tuna, tomato and cucumber to make sandwiches.

FISH IN A FOIL PACK

MAKES 4 SERVINGS

- 2 rainbow trout fillets or another tender fish* (about 1 lb.)
- 1 T. vegetable oil
- Garlic salt to taste
- Black pepper to taste
- Paprika to taste
- 1 jalapeño pepper, seeded, sliced
- 1 lemon, sliced

Preheat the grill to medium heat. Rinse fish and pat dry with paper towels. Rub fillets with oil and season with garlic salt, black pepper and paprika. Place each fillet on a 15-inch piece of sprayed aluminum foil. Top with jalapeño pepper slices and squeeze the juice from the ends of the lemon over the fish. Arrange lemon slices on top of fillets. Carefully fold all edges of foil to enclose fish and form a flat, airtight pack. Place foil packs on the grate over heat and cook for 15 to 20 minutes, without turning foil pack over, until fish flakes easily with a fork.

Try fillets of bass, flounder, perch or tilapia.

GRILLED SHRIMP PIZZA

MAKES 8 SERVINGS

> Juice from ½ fresh lime
> Juice from ½ fresh orange
> 1 T. honey
> 3 T. olive oil, divided
> 2 cloves garlic, minced
> 1 tsp. soy sauce
> ¼ tsp. black pepper
> ¼ C. chopped fresh cilantro
> 1 lb. large raw shrimp, peeled, deveined and rinsed

> 1 red and/or yellow bell pepper, quartered
> 1 small zucchini, cut lengthwise into
> ½" thick slices
> 1 lb. fresh pizza dough or frozen dough, thawed
> 1 (8 oz.) can pineapple chunks
> 2 C. shredded Monterey Jack cheese, divided

In a medium bowl, combine lime juice, orange juice, honey, 2 tablespoons oil, garlic, soy sauce, black pepper and cilantro; mix well. Divide mixture between two large resealable plastic bags. Add shrimp to one bag; add bell pepper and zucchini to other bag; seal and turn to coat food. Refrigerate bags to marinate shrimp and vegetables for 15 minutes.

To cook, lightly oil the grate and preheat grill to medium heat. Remove food and discard marinades. Thread shrimp on metal or soaked wooden skewers and grill for 5 to 8 minutes or until shrimp turn pink, flipping several times. Grill vegetables for 6 to 8 minutes or until tender-crisp; remove from grill and dice. Remove shrimp from skewers.

To assemble pizza, flatten dough to a 12 to 14 inches round, about ¼ inch thick. Brush dough with remaining 1 tablespoon oil. Place dough on the grate, oiled side down; cover grill. Cook for 1 to 2 minutes or until grill marks appear on bottom. Turn crust over with tongs or large spatula. Layer crust with half the cheese, grilled shrimp and vegetables; top with remaining cheese and pineapple. Cover grill and cook 3 to 4 minutes or until cheese melts and crust is brown. Check often and rotate as needed. Slide pizza onto a baking sheet to serve.

PERFECTLY GRILLED SCALLOPS

MAKES 4 SERVINGS

- 1 lb. sea scallops, approximately 1" thick*
- 2 T. olive oil
- Coarse salt to taste
- Coarsely ground black pepper to taste

Rinse scallops in cool water and pat dry thoroughly with paper towels, pressing down gently to remove moisture. Allow scallops to stand on paper towels for 10 minutes. Place scallops in a medium bowl and drizzle with oil; toss well to coat.

To cook, lightly oil the cleaned grate and preheat grill to medium-high heat. Thread approximately six scallops horizontally on each metal or soaked wooden skewer. Season with salt and black pepper. Place skewers on the grate directly over heat and cook for 1 to 2 minutes or until golden brown grill marks appear. Turn once and cook 1 to 2 minutes longer or until just cooked through. Remove from the grill and let stand for 2 to 3 minutes before serving. Slide scallops off skewers and serve warm.

If frozen, thaw completely and allow scallops to warm up to room temperature. Rinse and then pat dry several times. If scallops are big or thick, slice them in half horizontally before cooking.

SALMON SKEWERS

MAKES 12 SERVINGS

- 1 lb. skinless salmon filet
- 12 wooden skewers, soaked in water
- ¼ C. soy sauce
- ¼ C. honey
- 1 T. rice vinegar
- 1 tsp. minced fresh gingerroot
- 1 clove garlic, minced
- Pinch of pepper
- 12 lemon wedges

Lightly oil the grill grate and preheat grill to medium-high heat. Slice salmon filet lengthwise into 12 long strips and thread each strip on a soaked wooden skewer. Place skewers in a shallow baking dish. In a medium bowl, whisk together soy sauce, honey, vinegar, minced gingerroot, minced garlic, and pepper. Pour mixture over skewers in baking dish and let marinate at room temperature for 30 minutes. Pour remaining marinade into a small saucepan. Place saucepan over grill and bring mixture to a simmer. Thread 1 lemon wedge onto the end of each skewer. Place marinated skewers over heated grill and cook for 4 minutes on each side brushing often with simmering marinade mixture. Salmon is done when it flakes easily with a fork.

SHRIMP PACKS

MAKES 4 SERVINGS

- 1 (13.5 oz.) pkg. Andouille sausage
- 3 ears frozen or shucked fresh sweet corn
- 16 asparagus spears
- 1 lb. large peeled, cooked shrimp, tails removed
- 1 (8 oz.) pkg. sliced fresh mushrooms
- 1 or 2 lemons, sliced
- ¼ C. olive oil
- ¼ C. butter, sliced
- Salt, black pepper, & Old Bay seasoning to taste

Cut the sausage and corn into chunks and trim the ends off the asparagus spears.

Divide the cut-up food equally among four 18 x 24-inch sheets of heavy-duty foil that have been spritzed with cooking spray; add equal amounts of shrimp and mushrooms. Lay the lemon slices on top of the food. Drizzle each pack with 1 tablespoon oil; put pats of butter on top and sprinkle with salt, black pepper, and a generous amount of Old Bay. Double fold the tops and ends of the foil, sealing in the food and leaving some room inside for air to circulate.

Grill the packs over medium heat with the lid closed about 15 minutes, until the veggies are crisp-tender and shrimp are opaque, turning the packs once or twice. Open carefully to release steam away from your face.

GRILL PAN SALMON PATTIES

MAKES 4 TO 5 SERVINGS

- 1 (14.75 oz.) can salmon, drained & flaked
- 2 finely chopped green onions
- ½ C. finely diced red bell pepper
- 2 T. chopped fresh parsley
- 1 lightly beaten egg
- 2 T. lemon juice
- ¼ C. panko bread crumbs
- Sea salt & coarse black pepper to taste
- Guacamole

Mix the salmon, green onions, bell pepper, parsley, egg, lemon juice, bread crumbs, salt, and black pepper. Form into eight to ten (½ inch thick) firm patties; freeze for 15 minutes or chill for ½ hour. Set a grill pan on the grill and preheat on medium or medium-high heat. Coat the pan heavily with cooking spray. Add the chilled patties. Hear them sizzle? That's a good thing! Heat about 5 minutes on each side, flipping carefully when grill marks appear and the patties hold their shape. Top with some guacamole.

6 Breads

Grilling used to make me nervous, but then I learned to view the fire as just another source of heat, no different from a stove or an oven.
—*Samin Nosrat*

HOW TO GRILL FRENCH BREAD

To grill a bread loaf directly on the grate, preheat grill to medium heat. Slice loaf in half lengthwise; brush both cut and uncut sides of bread with olive oil. Grill on one side until light golden brown. Using tongs, turn the loaf over (at this point you can choose to remove the bread to a plate, add butters or toppings then return to grill topping side up) and grill until the second side is golden brown.

To grill thinly sliced bread directly on grate, preheat grill to medium heat. Slice a 1 pound loaf of French bread into ½-inch slices and brush both sides with oil. Lightly grill, about 1 minute per side.

To grill bread in foil, vertically cut French bread into 1-inch slices without cutting all the way through to the bottom, or cut horizontally the length of the bread. Preheat grill to medium heat. Mix butter and any seasonings and spread between the cuts in bread. Wrap in aluminum foil, bringing up sides and folding over to create a packet; place on grill. Close grill lid and bake about 15 minutes until heated through and butter has melted.

To grill bread on skewers, oil grate and preheat grill to medium heat. Slice French bread into bite-size cubes. In a large bowl, combine bread cubes and oil; toss to coat well. Evenly thread bread cubes onto skewers*, brush with additional oil. Close grill lid 5 to 8 minutes or until bread is lightly toasted, turning occasionally.

If using wooden skewers, be sure to soak in water at least 30 minutes before grilling to prevent burning.

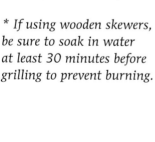

GRILLED BREAD & TOMATOES

MAKES 4 SERVINGS

- ¼ C. butter, melted
- 1 T. chopped garlic
- ½ loaf day-old French bread, cut into 1" slices
- 5 tomatoes, seeded and cut into chunks
- ½ red onion, finely chopped
- ¼ C. extra-virgin olive oil
- ¼ C. balsamic vinegar
- Salt and pepper to taste
- 1 T. coarsely chopped Italian parsley
- 1 T. coarsely chopped fresh basil leaves

Preheat the grill to medium-high. Melt the butter in a small saucepan; then add the chopped garlic. Brush the garlic butter on both sides of the bread slices. Grill the bread over medium-high heat until lightly browned, 3 to 4 minutes for each side.

Cut the grilled bread slices into quarters, and place them on a plate. Top with the chopped tomato and red onion. Drizzle the olive oil and balsamic vinegar over the top. Sprinkle with salt, pepper, parsley, and basil. Let stand about 30 minutes to allow the bread slices to absorb the liquids. Serve at room temperature.

FETA & OLIVE TOPPED FRENCH BREAD

MAKES ENOUGH FOR ONE 1 LB. LOAF

- ⅓ C. butter, softened
- ⅓ C. crumbled feta cheese
- ⅓ C. chopped black olives
- Sliced avocado, optional
- 1 loaf French bread, or bread of choice

In a small bowl, combine butter, cheese and olives. Spread over cut sides of partially grilled bread. Continue grilling, cheese side up, until cheese melts.

AVOCADO CHIMICHURRI BRUSCHETTA

MAKES 6 SERVINGS

- 2 ripe avocados
- ¼ C. parsley, chopped
- ¼ C. cilantro, chopped
- ½ shallot, finely diced
- 2 T. red wine vinegar
- 1 T. honey
- Olive oil, enough to bring everything together
- Salt and pepper to taste
- 6 slices thick Italian bread
- 1 garlic clove, peeled and cut in half

Cut the avocados in half; remove pits; and cut into cubes.

Combine avocados, parsley, cilantro, shallots, vinegar, honey, and olive oil. Season mixture with salt and pepper.

Brush olive oil on slices of bread, and grill on each side for a couple of minutes until toasted.

Rub the cut side of the garlic clove on grilled bread slices. Spread avocado mixture on bread, and serve immediately.

FRUIT BRUSCHETTA

MAKES APPROXIMATELY 24 SLICES

> 1 ½ C. chopped fresh strawberries, ¾ C. chopped, peeled fresh peaches, or other fruit as desired

> 1 ½ tsp. minced fresh mint

> 1 lb. loaf French bread, cut into ½" slices

> 2 T. olive oil

> ½ C. mascarpone cheese

In a medium bowl, combine strawberries, peaches and mint. Spread bread slices with olive oil and grill on one side. Remove from grill and spread grilled sides with cheese. Top cheese with fruit and grill 1 to 2 minutes more until cheese is slightly melted. Carefully remove from grill.

> Bruschetta consists of grilled bread rubbed with garlic, olive oil, salt and black pepper, but may include other seasonings and toppings. Bruschetta is usually served as a snack or appetizer and is delicious made on the grill.

BREAD PUDDING WITH DRIED CHERRIES

MAKES 6 SERVINGS

- 10 slices French bread (½" to 1" thick)
- 3 eggs
- 1¼ C. sugar
- 1½ tsp. vanilla extract
- 1¼ tsp. ground nutmeg
- 1¼ tsp. ground cinnamon
- 2 T. butter, melted
- 2 C. milk
- 1 C. dried cherries
- 1 tsp. finely grated lemon peel

Preheat grill to medium heat. Grill bread slices. Cut bread into cubes to equal 5 cups and set aside. In a large bowl, beat eggs until frothy, about 3 minutes. Add sugar, vanilla, nutmeg, cinnamon and butter. Blend well. Add milk; stir in dried cherries and lemon peel. Add bread cubes and toss until well combined. Let rest about 45 minutes, patting the bread down into the liquid occasionally. Transfer bread and egg mixture to a greased 5 x 9-inch foil loaf pan. Place pan in center of cooking grate, close lid and grill over indirect medium heat for 50 to 60 minutes or until top is well browned and puffy. Slice and serve warm.

HOW TO GRILL FLATBREAD

When a recipe calls for "flatbread," you can generally use any type of flatbread you wish. Some flatbreads are unleavened and some are made from dough or batter which uses yeast. While there are many types of flatbread, some of the more recognized types include pita, ciabatta, tortillas, focaccia and even bread dough or pizza dough. These recipes use purchased flatbreads, but you may substitute your favorite recipe for a homemade equivalent, if you choose. Experiment and enjoy.

Grilling unleavened (the "thin") flatbread is as easy as preheating the grill to medium heat and tossing the bread on the grill to lightly brown. Oil can be added, if desired. This type would include flatbreads like tortillas—both flour and corn—and pita bread. Of course, there are others, and it's fun to experiment with different types.

Grilling leavened (the "thick") flatbread is just as simple. Preheat grill to medium heat. Brush on a little oil and add a few seasonings to the bread, if you'd like, and grill until lightly toasted. Leavened flatbread could include ciabatta, focaccia and others like it.

Grilling leavened flatbread dough, such as pizza dough or bread dough, takes only a little more effort. Flatten dough to about ⅛ or ¼ inch thick and brush with oil. Preheat grill to high heat, then reduce heat to low or grill using indirect heat. Place dough on grill, oiled side down, and close the grill lid 2 or 3 minutes until bottom is lightly browned. Brush top side with oil, turn dough over (for toppings that need to heat, add them now) and grill with the lid closed for an additional 2 minutes or until that side is also lightly browned and any toppings are heated through.

CHEESY GRILLED CHICKEN QUESADILLAS

MAKES 12 SERVINGS

- 1 large grilled chicken breast, chopped
- 1 3-oz. package cream cheese, softened
- 1 C. shredded Monterey Jack cheese
- ⅓ C. crumbled feta cheese
- ½ tsp. dried oregano

- 4 large flour tortillas
- ⅓ C. chopped pitted ripe olives
- 2 T. diced pimento
- 2 T. thinly sliced green onion

For filling, stir together cream cheese, Monterey Jack, feta, and oregano. Spread ¼ of the filling onto half of each tortilla. Top with chicken, olives, pimento, and green onion. Fold plain side over; press gently to seal edges. Preheat grill to high; then reduce to medium. Place tortillas on grill, flipping once. When cheese has melted (about 5 to 8 minutes), remove and cut into three wedges. Serve immediately.

SMOKEY HOT CHILI-LIME CHALUPAS

MAKES ABOUT 5 SERVINGS

- 5 corn tortillas
- Vegetable oil for frying
- 1 C. refried beans, mashed
- 1 T. chili-lime rub
- ½ tsp. ground cumin

- 1 C. shredded Mexican cheese blend or Monterey Jack-Cheddar blend
- 15 slices fresh or pickled jalapeño peppers, optional
- Additional chili-lime rub, optional

Preheat grill to medium heat. Fry corn tortillas in hot oil, one at a time, until golden and crisp. In a medium bowl, combine beans, rub and cumin. Arrange tortillas on an aluminum tray. Spread bean mixture on each tortilla. Top with cheese, jalapeño pepper slices and additional chili-lime rub, if desired. Set tray over indirect heat, close grill lid and cook until cheese melts, about 15 minutes. Serve immediately.

PANZANELLA SKEWERS

- 24 (1½" to 2") cubes focaccia bread
- 1 tsp. dried basil
- 1 large clove garlic, minced
- 3 T. olive oil, divided

- 16 grape or cherry tomatoes
- 16 (1") chunks red onion
- ¼ C. pesto

Oil grate and preheat grill to medium heat. In a large bowl, combine bread cubes, basil and garlic. Drizzle with 2 tablespoons of the oil; toss to coat well. Evenly thread bread cubes, tomatoes and onions onto 8 skewers*. Brush with remaining oil. Place skewers on grate and close grill lid for 5 to 8 minutes or until bread is lightly toasted, turning occasionally. Remove from grill. Arrange on plates and drizzle with pesto.

* If using wooden skewers, be sure to soak in water at least 30 minutes before grilling to prevent burning.

HOT GARLIC BREAD

MAKES 16 SERVINGS

- 1 C. butter
- 5 ½ T. minced garlic
- 2 ½ T. crumbled blue cheese
- 3 ½ T. mixed herbs
- 1 T. crushed red pepper flakes
- Sea salt and pepper to taste
- Dash of Worcestershire sauce
- 1 thin baguette, cut into thick slices

Preheat grill to high heat. Place a medium saucepan over grill. Place butter in the saucepan until melted and stir in minced garlic, crumbled blue cheese, mixed herbs, red pepper flakes, sea salt, pepper, and Worcestershire sauce. Mix well until thoroughly heated through. Dunk baguette slices in melted butter mixture to coat both sides. Place coated baguette slices over grill and toast for 1 minute on each side, brushing with any remaining butter mixture.

BEER-CHEESEWICHES

MAKES 6 SANDWICHES

- 3 C. shredded sharp cheddar cheese
- 1 C. shredded Swiss cheese
- 1 T. Worcestershire sauce
- 1 tsp. dry mustard

- ¼ tsp. cayenne pepper
- ¼ tsp. salt
- ½ (12 oz.) bottle of Pilsner
- 12 slices Texas toast

Preheat the grill on low heat. Stir together shredded sharp cheddar cheese, shredded Swiss cheese, Worcestershire sauce, dry mustard, cayenne pepper, and salt. Slowly stir in the Pilsner, until the cheese is just barely moistened. Divide the cheese mixture among 6 slices of Texas toast; spread evenly but not all the way to the edges. Put another slice of bread over the cheese and squish together. Spread a little melted butter over both sides of the sandwiches and arrange on the grill. Close the lid, but don't walk away. In just a couple of minutes, peak at the bottom. When you see golden brown, flip and repeat. Enjoy immediately, but watch out for the molten cheese flow.

ONE-BEER SKILLET BREAD

MAKES 12 SERVINGS

> 3 C. self-rising flour
> ¼ C. sugar
> Pinch salt
> 1 can beer
> 1 egg, beaten

OPTIONAL ADDITIONS
> Sliced onions, corn, bacon bits, bell pepper, jalapeño, or chopped herbs

Preheat grill to medium low. Mix flour, sugar, salt, and beer, and lightly knead into a dough. Pour dough into a well-seasoned cast-iron skillet, or add a bit of bacon grease to the bottom and sides of a pan. Brush the top of the dough with the beaten egg; then top with the onions, corn, or other additions.

Place skillet on grill over indirect heat. Close lid. After about 50 minutes, move the skillet over direct heat, and continue cooking for 10 minutes.

Skillet bread is done when toothpick inserted in the center comes out clean. Flip bread over onto a cooling rack. Serve in wedges.

DILL-ICIOUS RYE PULL-APART

SERVES A CROWD

- 1 (1 lb.) round loaf rye bread
- 8 oz. shredded dill Havarti cheese
- ½ lb. dried beef (aka smoked beef), chopped
- ½ C. unsalted butter, melted
- 1 to 2 T. dry ranch dressing mix
- Dill weed to taste

Preheat the grill on medium-low heat for indirect cooking. Cut the bread from the top down in ¾-inch-wide lengthwise and crosswise slices, without cutting through the bottom; set on a large sheet of heavy-duty foil and roll the foil up around the sides of the bread, creating a nest to hold the bread in place. Set aside ¼ of the cheese and push the remainder into the cuts of the bread along with all the beef. Stir together the butter and ranch dressing mix and drizzle evenly over the top. Sprinkle the set-aside cheese and the dill weed over all. Cover with a piece of foil and place the loaf on the cool side of the grill. Close the lid and cook 12 to 15 minutes, rotating once or twice. Remove the top piece of foil, close the lid again, and cook 12 to 15 minutes longer, rotating occasionally.

HOT HONEY CORNBREAD SLABS

SERVINGS VARY

> 8.5 oz. pkg. of corn muffin mix
> ½ C. softened butter

> 1 finely diced jalapeño
> 2 T. honey

Make an 8.5 oz. pkg. of corn muffin mix according to package directions and bake in an 8 x 8-inch pan (or whip up a batch using your favorite recipe). Let cool, then cut into squares (if more than ¾ inch thick, slice in half horizontally,too). Beat together butter, jalapeño, and honey. Preheat the grill on medium-high heat. Coat the cornbread slices with cooking spray and set on the grill for a couple of minutes on each side, until crispy. Spread the butter mixture on the cornbread and serve immediately.

ULTIMATE GRILLED CUBAN LOAF

MAKES 4 SERVINGS

- ⅓ C. melted butter
- 1 (1 lb.) loaf Italian bread, halved lengthwise
- 8 salami slices
- 8 tomato slices
- Sliced onions
- 8 to 10 kosher baby dill pickles, halved lengthwise
- About 5 oz. each sliced Gruyère, fontina, and American cheeses

Preheat the grill on low heat. Brush butter over cut side of each bread half and set them on the grill, cut side down. Heat until light golden brown. Remove from the grill and flip them over onto a big piece of foil. To the bottom bread half, add layers of salami, tomato, onion, pickles, and all three cheeses. Plop the top bread half on the sandwich and wrap the foil tightly around it to hold all those layers in place, leaving the ends open. Return the loaf to the grill and set a heavy pan on top; heat about 8 minutes on each side, until the cheese is melted and gooey. Take it off the grill, slice it up, and enjoy.

7 Fruit

People get a little bolder and more wild in summer. . . .
There's something about standing over a grill
or outside with the family that inspires us.
—*Guy Fieri*

HOW TO GRILL APPLES & PEARS

Apples and pears share a common texture and mild flavor. Firmer types of fruit (Bosc pears, for example), should be used for grilling. Both apples and pears can be stuffed and grilled in foil, skewered or grilled directly on the grates.

To grill whole apples or pears, remove core from each piece of fruit without cutting through to the bottom, forming a cavity. Preheat grill to medium heat. Set fruit cored-side-up on heavy-duty aluminum foil. Add 1 teaspoon butter and a sprinkle of cinnamon and sugar to each cavity or stuff with filling. To grill, wrap securely in aluminum foil, folding ends over, leaving a little space for air circulation. Grill, seam side up, about 10 minutes or until fruit is slightly tender.

To grill rings of fruit, remove stem and blossom ends and slice the remainder of the fruit into crosswise slices, about ½ inch thick, removing seeds and core. Preheat grill to medium heat. Place rings, cut side down, directly on grate or use a grill basket. Grill until lightly browned. Using a spatula or tongs, carefully turn rings and grill the other side until brown. Fruit rings can also be wrapped in heavy-duty aluminum foil, folding ends of foil over and leaving a little space for air circulation. Grill, seam side up, until fruit is tender.

To grill fruit halves or wedges, slice fruit in half vertically and remove core and stem. Further slice into wedges, if desired. Preheat grill to medium heat. Place cut side down on grate. Grill both sides until lightly browned, turning carefully with a spatula or tongs. Fruit can also be grilled in a grill basket or wrapped in heavy-duty aluminum foil as described above.

To grill on skewers, slice fruit in half, removing core and stem. Slice each half into chunks or thick slices and thread onto skewers*. Preheat grill to medium heat. Place skewers on grate, turning occasionally until fruit is lightly browned and softened.

If using wooden skewers, be sure to soak in water at least 30 minutes before using to prevent burning.

HOW TO GRILL BANANAS

To grill bananas in their skins, leave whole, slice in half horizontally or cut through the top of the peel and banana without cutting through the bottom. If whole, just place on a grill preheated to medium heat with lid closed, grilling for about 3 to 5 minutes, turning occasionally. If cut, place on a grill preheated to medium heat and grill, cut side up, closing the lid and grilling until bananas begin to pull away from the peel, 3 to 5 minutes. Cutting allows you to easily stuff with filling. The fruit will be soft, so remove carefully from peels.

To grill without skins, place whole or cut bananas in a foil pan or on heavy-duty aluminum foil. Preheat grill to medium heat. Fold foil around bananas but do not seal or cover pan. Grill for about 10 minutes or until bananas are tender.

To grill on skewers, cut bananas into 1½-inch chunks. Thread onto skewers, brush with oil or butter and add spices, if desired. Preheat grill to medium heat and grill for about 5 minutes on each side, brushing occasionally with oil or butter. Do not overcook.

HOW TO GRILL PINEAPPLE

Grilling pineapple brings out its sugars and creates a wonderfully sweet treat to eat alone or along with other foods. If you haven't tried grilling this tropical fruit, be sure to add it to your "To Do" list.

To grill pineapple wedges, cut bottom and top off pineapple; stand up on end and slice downward, rotating pineapple, until outer skin is completely removed. Slice pineapple, from the top down around core to create long thick wedges. Preheat grill to medium heat. Brush wedges with oil, glaze or marinade and place on grill that has been preheated to medium heat until browned grill marks form. Turn wedges over and grill until all sides are browned.

To grill pineapple slices, remove outer skin from pineapple as directed above and cut into ½-inch slices or rings. Brush with oil, glaze or marinade and place on grill that has been preheated to medium heat. Grill until nicely browned on both sides.

To grill on skewers, cut pineapple wedges or slices into chunks and thread onto skewers. Brush with oil, glaze or marinade, if desired, and again, grill until evenly browned on all sides.

To grill in aluminum foil, place pineapple in heavy-duty aluminum foil (or in a foil pan covered with foil) sprayed with nonstick cooking spray. Add sauces, marinades or olive oil, if desired. Preheat grill to medium heat. Using indirect heat, grill for 5 to 10 minutes until tender. Grilling in foil produces a softer texture than grilling directly on the grate.

GRILLED APPLES STUFFED WITH OATMEAL

MAKES 4 SERVINGS

- ❭ 4 apples (McIntosh, Fuji, or Golden Delicious)
- ❭ ½ C. oatmeal, plain (instant)
- ❭ 1½ C. water
- ❭ ½ banana (very ripe, pureed)
- ❭ 1 tsp. ground cinnamon
- ❭ ⅛ tsp. ground nutmeg
- ❭ ⅛ tsp. ground cloves
- ❭ 1 tsp. vanilla extract
- ❭ 8 walnuts, coarsely ground
- ❭ 1 T. light brown sugar
- ❭ 1–2 lemon slices

Begin by cooking the oatmeal on your stove (medium-high heat). Bring the water to a boil; stir in the oatmeal; add the banana, cinnamon, nutmeg, cloves, vanilla, light brown sugar, and walnuts. Cook for 1 minute, stirring regularly. Cover, and remove from heat.

Trim a thin slice off of the bottom of each apple (keeping it level). Cut off the top of the apple, and using a small paring knife, hollow out the apple to create a cavity for the oatmeal filling.

Preheat one side of grill to medium. Rub the cut parts of the apples with a lemon slice (to keep from browning). Stuff the apples with oatmeal filling; place them on the grill over indirect heat; and close the grill. (The apples will cook more evenly.) Cook for 20–25 minutes.

GRILLED PEAR SALAD

MAKES ABOUT 6 SERVINGS

- 2 T. brown sugar
- ¼ tsp. black pepper
- 2 T. chopped walnuts
- 2 pears, cored and cut into 6 lengthwise wedges
- Lemon juice for brushing

- 2 T. fresh lemon juice
- 1 T. rice vinegar
- 1 tsp. Dijon mustard
- 1 T. minced shallot
- ¼ tsp. salt
- ¼ tsp. black pepper

- 1 T. olive oil
- 6 C. watercress sprigs or other leafy greens, tough stems removed
- 3 T. crumbled blue cheese

In a small pan over medium heat, combine brown sugar, 1 tablespoon water and black pepper. Cook, stirring constantly, until sugar dissolves. Stir in walnuts; reduce heat to low and cook for 30 seconds. Remove from heat and quickly spread nuts on a sheet of parchment paper or a plate. Set aside to cool. Brush the pear wedges with lemon juice and grill over medium heat until pears begin to brown, 3 to 4 minutes, turning once. Set aside. To make the vinaigrette, in a small bowl, whisk together 2 tablespoons lemon juice, vinegar, mustard and shallot. Add salt and black pepper; whisk to blend. While whisking, slowly add the oil in a thin stream until emulsified. In a large bowl, combine watercress and cheese; add vinaigrette and toss gently to mix well and coat evenly. To serve, divide the salad among individual plates. Place two pear wedges on each and sprinkle with candied walnuts.

GRILLED FRUIT OVER YOGURT

MAKES 4 SERVINGS

- 2 bananas, peeled and left whole
- ¼ pineapple, cut into 1" cubes
- 2 plums, pitted and cut in half lengthwise
- 8 strawberries, tops cut off, left whole
- 1 peach, pitted and cut in half lengthwise
- 4 C. vanilla nonfat Greek yogurt (or your favorite flavor)

Preheat grill to medium high. Grill all of the fruit. (Use skewers if that's easier; remember to soak the skewers in water first to prevent burning.) Take the fruit off of the grill. Cut the bananas and the peaches into four equal pieces. Mix all of the fruit together, and serve over the yogurt.

BACON MAPLE BANANA BITES

MAKES 8 SERVINGS

- ⟩ 2 large bananas
- ⟩ 1 tsp. chili powder, or to taste
- ⟩ ¼ C. maple syrup
- ⟩ 8 strips center-cut bacon

Lightly oil or spray grates with nonstick cooking spray. Preheat grill to medium heat. Pour maple syrup into shallow dish; place bacon on a microwave-safe plate lined with paper towels. Cover with another paper towel and microwave on high 1 minute or until bacon just begins to cook, but is still pliable. Peel bananas and sprinkle with chili powder; cut each into four equal pieces. Roll pieces in maple syrup and wrap in one strip of bacon. Secure with toothpicks. Place on grill, close lid and heat 5 to 8 minutes or until bacon is browned and crisp, turning occasionally.

GRILLED PEANUT-BUTTER-AND-BANANA SANDWICHES

MAKES 4 SERVINGS

> 8 slices multi-grain bread of your choice
> ½ C. natural peanut butter
> 2 large bananas

> 2 T. clover honey
> 4 pinches salt
> Cooking spray as needed

Preheat one side of grill to low. Make four peanut-butter-and-banana sandwiches by adding 1 tablespoon of peanut butter to each slice of bread. To that add a half banana per sandwich, sliced lengthwise. Drizzle each sandwich with ½ tablespoon of honey and a pinch of salt.

Apply cooking spray as needed to the grill, and place each sandwich at a 45-degree angle to the grates. After 1 or 2 minutes rotate the sandwich 90 degrees. When browned, flip each sandwich and repeat. Serve sliced into triangles.

SPICED GRILLED BANANAS

MAKES ABOUT 4 SERVINGS

- 3 large, firm bananas, peeled
- ¼ C. golden raisins, optional
- 3 T. brown sugar
- ½ tsp. ground cinnamon
- ¼ tsp. ground nutmeg
- ¼ tsp. ground cardamom or coriander
- 2 T. butter, cut into 8 pieces
- 1 T. fresh lime juice
- Frozen vanilla yogurt
- Additional fresh lime juice
- Toppings as desired

Preheat grill to low heat. Spray 9-inch disposable foil pan with nonstick cooking spray. Cut bananas in half lengthwise or diagonally into ½-inch-thick slices. Overlap in prepared pan. Sprinkle with raisins. In a small bowl, combine sugar, cinnamon, nutmeg and cardamom; sprinkle over bananas and raisins. Dot with butter. Cover pie plate tightly with foil. Place on grate, close grill lid and cook over low heat 10 to 15 minutes or until bananas are hot and tender. Carefully remove foil and sprinkle with lime juice. Serve over frozen yogurt and sprinkle with additional lime juice or nuts and caramel sauce.

WATERMELON & FETA SKEWERS

MAKES 4 SERVINGS

- ❯ ½ fresh watermelon, cut into 1½" x 1½" x 5" blocks
- ❯ 1 lime, juiced
- ❯ Salt and pepper to taste
- ❯ Cooking spray as needed
- ❯ 4 bamboo skewers, soaked in water

FETA CHEESE MIX
- ❯ ½ C. feta cheese
- ❯ ½ C. peeled and finely diced cucumber
- ❯ ¼ C. thinly sliced fresh spearmint leaves
- ❯ 1 T. rice or champagne vinegar
- ❯ Salt and pepper to taste

Preheat grill to medium. Place a presoaked skewer into the end of the watermelon; drizzle with lime, salt, and pepper; and spray with cooking spray. Grill to desired doneness.

In a bowl, mix the cheese, cucumber, mint, and vinegar, and then season. To serve, place one piece of watermelon on a plate and top with a spoonful of the cheese mix.

GRILLED WATERMELON & WATERCRESS SALAD

MAKES 4 SERVINGS

- 4 large watermelon slices
- 2 bunches (about 2 C.) watercress, rinsed
- 2 T. olive oil
- ½ lemon, juiced
- Salt and pepper to taste
- Cooking spray as needed

Preheat grill to high. Spray the hottest part of the grill with the cooking spray, and carefully place the melon slices at a 45-degree angle to the grills. Because of the high moisture content, the slices will take several minutes to mark, depending on the heat of your grill. Do not move them until they are done. When one side is marked, flip and repeat on the other side.

In a bowl, mix the oil, lemon juice, and watercress, tossing to coat. Season the coated watercress with salt and pepper, and place on four plates. Top each watercress pile with a slice of the grilled watermelon, and serve.

FIRECRACKER WATERMELON

SERVINGS VARY

- 1 mini watermelon
- Salt and black pepper
- Lime juice
- Honey
- Jalapeño slices, feta cheese, cilantro (toppings)

Grease the grill rack and preheat the grill on medium high heat. In the meantime, cut 1 mini watermelon into 1-inch-thick slices; cut each slice into four even pieces and sprinkle with salt and black pepper. Set the melon on the hot grill rack and cook for a few minutes on each side until grill marks appear; set aside to cool slightly. At serving time, drizzle the slices with lime juice and honey. Top with jalapeño slices, crumbled feta cheese, and fresh cilantro.

TEQUILA-LIME SALSA

MAKES 6 CUPS

- 2 firm ripe mangoes
- 1 pineapple, peeled
- 1 red bell pepper
- 3 T. melted unsalted butter
- ⅔ C. chopped red onion
- ¼ C. chopped fresh cilantro
- Juice of ½ lime
- ⅛ tsp. black pepper
- 1 T. agave nectar
- 2 T. tequila
- 1½ tsp. smoked paprika

Slice off the two fat sides of each mango; cut a crisscross pattern into the fruit slices without cutting through the skin. Core the pineapple and cut into six wedges. Cut the bell pepper into thirds; remove the stem and seeds. Grease the grill rack and preheat the grill on medium heat. Brush the mango, pineapple, and pepper pieces with butter and arrange on the hot grill rack. Cook everything until grill marks appear, flipping the pineapple and pepper to brown all sides. Set all aside to cool. Use a spoon to remove the mango pieces from the skin; toss the pieces into a bowl. Cut the pineapple and pepper into bite-size pieces and add to the bowl along with the onion, cilantro, lime juice, pepper, agave nectar, tequila, and paprika. Stir until well blended. Serve with tortilla chips or use as a condiment for grilled burgers.

8 Vegetables

Grilling takes the formality out of entertaining.
Everyone wants to get involved.
—*Bobby Flay*

ROASTED ASPARAGUS WITH CHERRY TOMATOES, GARLIC & OLIVE OIL

MAKES 4 SERVINGS

- 2 lbs. pencil asparagus, woody ends trimmed
- 2 C. washed and stemmed cherry tomatoes
- 12 garlic cloves, peeled and smashed
- ¼ C. extra-virgin olive oil
- 1 tsp. coarse salt
- ½ tsp. freshly ground black pepper
- ¼ C. fresh lemon juice, reserve lemon halves

Preheat the grill to medium high. In a large bowl, combine the asparagus, tomatoes, and garlic. Drizzle with the olive oil, and season with the coarse salt and pepper. Toss to coat; then transfer to a large aluminum baking sheet. Drizzle the lemon juice over the asparagus; add the lemon halves to the pan; and place on the grill. Roast until the asparagus stalks are tender and the tomatoes begin to caramelize, about 20 to 25 minutes. Remove from the grill, and serve hot or at room temperature.

GARLIC-GRILLED PORTOBELLOS

MAKES 4 SERVINGS

- 4 portobello mushrooms, about 1 lb.
- ⅓ C. extra-virgin olive oil
- 3 T. lemon juice
- 2 cloves garlic, peeled and minced
- Salt and pepper to taste
- 2 T. minced fresh parsley

Preheat the grill to medium-high. Brush any dirt or grit off the mushrooms with a damp paper towel. Remove the stems. Combine the oil, lemon juice, and garlic in a bowl. Brush the caps on both sides with the garlic oil; sprinkle salt and pepper on both sides, and let them stand for 15 minutes, stem side up. Place the caps on a well-oiled grill, stem side up; grill them for 3 to 4 minutes. Turn the caps over, and grill them for another 3 to 4 minutes or until easily pierced with a knife. Do not burn or overcook them; the centers should be tender and moist. Transfer the caps to a platter, and cut them into thick slices. Garnish with parsley before serving.

GRILLED RATATOUILLE

MAKES 4 SERVINGS

- ½ large red onion, quartered
- 1 package cherry tomatoes
- 2 zucchini, sliced
- 1 package sliced mushrooms
- 2 large yellow squash, sliced
- 1 red pepper, julienned
- 1 yellow pepper, julienned
- 1 green pepper, julienned
- ¾ C. balsamic vinegar
- ¼ C. Worcestershire sauce
- 1 T. olive oil
- 1 T. Creole seasoning
- 1 tsp. seasoned salt

Combine ingredients in a large bowl; then in a plastic storage bag. Marinate in the refrigerator for at least 2 hours. Preheat grill to medium-high. Grill the mixture in a grill wok or a basket until the vegetables are tender, stirring occasionally. The vegetables are best when somewhat charred.

GRILLED EGGPLANT WITH CHEESE

MAKES ABOUT 4 TO 6 SERVINGS

- 4 small eggplants
- Olive oil
- Salt and pepper
- ½ lb. soft goat cheese or feta, crumbled
- 2 tsp. garlic, minced
- 1 tsp. red pepper flakes
- 1 T. fresh basil, finely chopped

Cut eggplants in half lengthwise. Brush cut edges with olive oil, and season with salt and pepper. In a small bowl, combine cheese, garlic, red pepper flakes, and basil with a pinch of salt, and then refrigerate until ready to use. Preheat the grill to medium. Place eggplant halves on grill over direct heat, skinless side down. Roast until almost soft (2 to 3 minutes). Remove from grill, and cool slightly. Then spread or sprinkle the cheese mixture on the warm eggplant, and serve immediately.

CRAB-STUFFED MUSHROOMS

MAKES 12 SERVINGS

- 12 fresh small mushrooms
- 1 (8 oz.) pkg. cream cheese, softened
- 1 cluster of steamed crab meat, cut into small pieces
- 3 cloves garlic, chopped
- 4 oz. shredded mozzarella cheese
- 4 oz. Asiago cheese

Preheat grill to medium heat. Remove and chop mushroom stems. In a large bowl, combine cream cheese, crab meat, garlic and stems. Stuff mushrooms with cream cheese mixture. In a small bowl, combine mozzarella and Asiago cheeses; dip stuffed side of each mushroom into the mixture. Place mushrooms, stuffing side up, on a disposable foil pan or heavy-duty aluminum foil which has been sprayed with nonstick cooking spray. Grill with lid closed until cheese is melted.

STUFFED TOMATOES ON THE GRILL

MAKES 6 SERVINGS

- 6 large tomatoes
- Ketchup to taste
- 1½ C. herb-seasoned stuffing
- ½ C. grated Romano cheese
- 2 T. chopped scallion
- Dash pepper
- 2 T. butter, melted

Preheat the grill to medium-high. Slice the top portion from each tomato; discard. Scoop out the pulp from each tomato. Chop and drain the pulp. Turn the tomato shells upside down on a paper towel to drain them.

In a bowl, combine the chopped tomato pulp, ketchup to taste, stuffing mix, cheese, scallion, pepper, and butter. Lightly salt the tomato shells; fill them with stuffing mixture. Wrap the bottom of each tomato in aluminum foil. Grill for about 30 minutes.

SPICY GRILLED FRIES

MAKES 4 TO 6 SERVINGS

- 1 T. paprika
- 1 tsp. freshly ground black pepper
- 1 tsp. kosher salt
- ½ tsp. chili powder
- Pinch of cayenne (optional)
- 4 large russet or baking potatoes, scrubbed but not peeled
- Olive oil

Preheat the grill to medium low. Combine the first five ingredients in a small bowl. Cut the potatoes in half lengthwise; then slice each half into long wedges that are about ½ inch thick in the middle. Place the potatoes in a large plastic storage bag, and pour the oil on top. Shake well to coat; then sprinkle the potatoes generously with the spice mixture, and shake again until they are well coated. Place the potatoes directly on the grate, and grill for 30 to 35 minutes, turning every 5 to 7 minutes. Dab them lightly with additional oil as needed. The potatoes are ready when crisp and golden brown outside and soft in the middle.

GRILLED RED POTATOES & GREEN BEANS WITH PESTO

MAKES 4 SERVINGS

- 1 lb. fresh green beans, rinsed and trimmed
- 2 C. water
- 12 red potatoes (about 1½ lbs.)
- Nonstick vegetable oil spray
- 2½ C. basil leaves
- ¼ C. chopped Italian parsley
- 2 T. olive oil
- ⅓ C. vegetable broth
- 2 large garlic cloves, peeled and halved
- ¼ C. pine nuts
- ¼ C. grated Parmesan cheese

Steam beans in microwave or steamer basket on stovetop until almost tender, about 8 minutes. Transfer beans to bowl of ice water to stop cooking. Drain beans, and cut them in half.

Preheat grill. Thread three red potatoes onto each of four skewers. Spray the potatoes and grill with oil. Place the skewers on the grill. Turning as needed, grill 20 to 30 minutes or until potatoes are tender. Remove potatoes from grill; set aside. When cool enough to handle, remove potatoes from skewers, and cut each potato in half. Set aside.

To make pesto, combine basil, parsley, olive oil, broth, garlic, pine nuts, and Parmesan in a food processor or blender. Blend until ingredients resemble a sauce. Transfer to a bowl.

While grill is still hot, place wire basket on grill; lightly oil basket; and then add potatoes and beans. Place basket on grill, and heat, tossing frequently, 4 to 5 minutes. Remove from grill, and divide mixture among four plates. Serve with pesto.

GRILLED CORN WITH SUN-DRIED TOMATO PESTO

MAKES 4 SERVINGS

- 4 ears of corn in husks
- ½ C. sun-dried tomatoes
- 2 T. whole pine nuts

- ¼ C. olive oil
- 1 tsp. chopped garlic
- Salt and pepper to taste

Soak the corn in water for 45 minutes to 1 hour. Place the remaining ingredients in a blender; puree until smooth.

Preheat grill to medium. Remove the corn from the water. Peel back the husks, leaving them attached at the stem. Grill the corn for 8 to 10 minutes, turning often. Remove from the grill, and spread the corn with the sun-dried pesto. Serve immediately.

EASY HERBED POTATOES

MAKES 4 TO 6 SERVINGS

- 2 T. olive oil
- 1 T. balsamic vinegar
- 1 tsp. garlic salt
- 1 tsp. dried rosemary
- ¼ tsp. pepper

- 2 small Vidalia onions, peeled and cut into wedges
- 3 large carrots, peeled and sliced diagonally
- 2 red potatoes, chopped

Preheat grill to high heat or oven to 400°F. In a 9 x 13-inch metal baking dish, combine olive oil, vinegar, garlic salt, dried rosemary, and pepper. Add onion wedges, carrot slices and chopped potatoes. Toss until evenly coated. Place baking dish directly over grill, cover grill, and cook, turning occasionally, until vegetables are tender.

CARROTS WITH A SNAP

MAKES 4 SERVINGS

- 32 baby carrots or 8 regular carrots, cut into 2" pieces
- ½ jalapeño pepper, seeded and chopped
- ¼ tsp. unsalted butter
- Salt and black pepper to taste

Place eight baby carrots each on four pieces of heavy-duty foil. Add the chopped pepper and butter to each; then add salt and pepper to taste. Fold up the edges of each piece of foil to create a tight seal to form packets. Grill the packets over medium heat, turning once, for 20 to 25 minutes.

FIRE-ROASTED CAESAR SALAD

MAKES 6 SERVINGS

- 1 clove garlic
- Salt
- 1 T. lemon juice
- 1 T. mayonnaise
- 1 tsp. anchovy paste
- 1 tsp. Dijon mustard
- 1 tsp. each Worcestershire sauce & Tabasco sauce
- 1 tsp. distilled white vinegar
- ¼ C. grated Parmesan cheese
- ¼ C. olive oil, plus more for brushing
- Black pepper to taste
- 3 Romaine lettuce hearts
- Shredded Parmesan cheese

In a bowl, mash together the garlic and ⅛ teaspoon salt to form a paste. Stir in the lemon juice, mayonnaise, anchovy paste, mustard, Worcestershire sauce, Tabasco sauce, vinegar, and the grated Parmesan. Add the oil in a slow, steady stream while whisking rapidly. Season with pepper and chill until serving time. Preheat the grill and a grill pan on high heat. Cut the Romaine hearts in half lengthwise, brush with oil, and sprinkle with a little salt and pepper. Set the Romaine halves on the hot pan and grill until nicely charred and wilted, turning occasionally. Serve with the chilled dressing and top with some shredded Parmesan.

ATOMIC POPPERS

- 10 jalapeños
- 8 oz. cream cheese spread
- 1 C. Monterey Jack cheese, finely shredded
- 1 tsp. chipotle powder
- 2 green onions, finely chopped
- 10 mini smoked sausages
- 10 bacon strips, cooked

Preheat the grill on medium-low heat. Slice 10 jalapeños in half lengthwise; remove and discard the seeds and membranes. (Always be careful prepping jalapeños—these beasts can do a number on your skin and eyes.) Mix an 8 ounce tub of cream cheese spread with 1 cup finely shredded Monterey Jack cheese, 1 teaspoon chipotle powder, and 2 finely chopped green onions; stuff into the pepper halves. Nestle a mini smoked sausage into the filling of each and wrap a cooked bacon strip around the whole thing. Secure with toothpicks and set them on the grill; close the lid and cook several minutes, until the peppers are slightly tender and lightly charred and the filling is piping hot.

BIG BITE VEGGIE SANDWICHES

MAKES 6 SERVINGS

- 1 eggplant, sliced ⅜" thick
- Coarse salt
- ⅔ C. olive oil
- 2 tsp. minced garlic
- 2 bell peppers, any color
- 2 yellow summer squash, sliced ½" thick

- 1 red onion, sliced ½" thick
- 8 oz. whole mushrooms
- Coarse black pepper
- 12 (½"-thick) slices ciabatta bread
- Italian salad dressing

- 12 slices provolone cheese
- Fresh spinach
- 3 large tomatoes, sliced
- Fresh basil

Preheat the grill on medium-high heat. Sprinkle both sides of eggplant slices with salt and set on a wire rack for 20 minutes; pat dry. Mix the oil and garlic and brush some all over the peppers; set on the hot grill rack until blistered on all sides, turning occasionally. Transfer to a zippered plastic freezer bag; seal and set aside. Brush eggplant, squash, onion, and mushrooms with the remaining oil; sprinkle with salt and pepper. Arrange veggies on the grill and cook 10 minutes or until grill marks appear on both sides, flipping once. Remove from the grill; slice the mushrooms. Remove the charred skin from the set-aside peppers; cut into strips and remove seeds. Coat both sides of the bread slices with cooking spray, arrange on the grill, and cook until the bottoms are toasted; flip, drizzle with salad dressing, top each with a provolone slice, and toast the other side. Layer half the bread slices with grilled veggies, spinach, tomatoes, and basil; top with another bread slice.

HASSELBACK SWEET POTATOES

MAKES 2 SERVINGS

- 1 T. butter, melted
- 1 tsp. minced garlic
- ⅛ tsp. each cayenne pepper, sweet paprika, and black pepper
- ¼ tsp. salt
- 1 tsp. canola oil, plus more for coating
- 2 medium sweet potatoes
- ½ C. crumbled feta cheese
- A big handful of roasted & salted pistachios, shelled & chopped

In a small bowl, mix butter, garlic, cayenne, paprika, black pepper, salt, and 1 teaspoon oil; set aside. Cut off a thin lengthwise slice from the bottom of each sweet potato so it sets flat; cut off pointed ends. Lay a sweet potato lengthwise between two wooden spoon handles. Use a knife to make ⅛-inch-wide cuts into the top of the sweet potato until the knife hits the spoons. Repeat with other sweet potato. Rinse, pat dry, and set on a microwave-safe plate. Microwave on high for 3 minutes; flip and microwave 3 minutes longer. Preheat the grill on medium heat, for indirect cooking. Brush the sweet potatoes with oil, place in a foil pan, and set the pan on the cool side of the grill. Close the lid and cook for 10 minutes. Spread the set-aside butter mixture over the top and between the slices of the sweet potatoes; close the lid and cook 10 minutes longer, until soft in the center. Top with feta and pistachios.

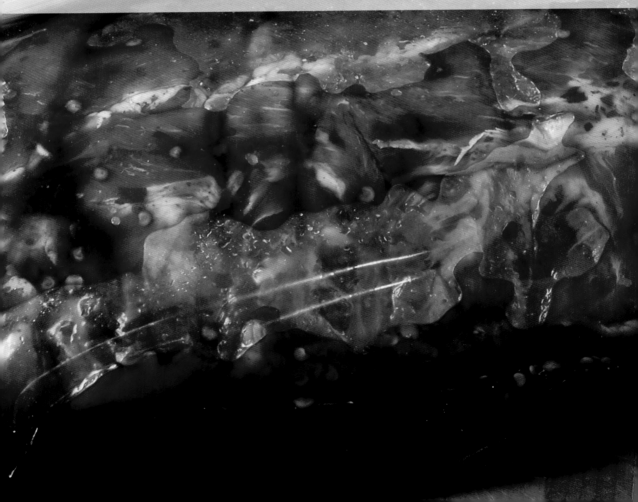

9 Sauces, Marinades, Rubs & Glazes

There are two different things: there's grilling, and there's barbecue. Grilling is when people say, "We're going to turn up the heat, make it really hot, and sear a steak, sear a burger." Barbecue is going low and slow.

—Guy Fieri

SPICE RUB FOR CHICKEN

MAKES ABOUT ⅓ CUP

- 3 T. paprika
- 1 T. ground cumin
- 1 T. dry mustard
- 2 tsp. ground fennel seeds
- 1 tsp. salt
- 1 tsp. black pepper
- Canola oil for brushing

In a small bowl, combine paprika, cumin, dry mustard, fennel, salt and pepper; mix well. Lightly brush both sides of each chicken breast half with canola oil. Rub the top of each piece with spice mixture and place on a lightly oiled grate over direct heat, rub side down; cook for 4 to 5 minutes or until golden brown and crusty. Turn chicken over and continue to grill for 10 minutes or until cooked through.

ASIAN MARINADE FOR CHICKEN

MARINATES 4 CHICKEN BREAST HALVES

- ½ C. olive oil
- ½ C. white grape juice
- ½ C. reduced-sodium soy sauce
- ½ C. chopped green onion
- 3 T. sesame seeds, toasted*
- 1 T. dry mustard
- 1 T. grated fresh gingerroot
- 1 tsp. black pepper
- 4 cloves garlic, minced

In a large resealable plastic bag, combine oil, grape juice, soy sauce, green onion, sesame seeds, dry mustard, gingerroot, black pepper and garlic; mix well. Set aside ½ cup of sauce for basting during grilling; cover and refrigerate. Add chicken to remaining mixture in bag, seal and turn bag to coat meat; refrigerate bag to marinate chicken for 4 to 6 hours. To cook, drain and discard marinade. Grill chicken, using the reserved marinade to baste meat several times toward the end of cooking.

To toast, place sesame seeds in a dry skillet over medium heat and cook until browned, about 3 to 5 minutes, shaking pan often.

TROPICAL MARINADE FOR CHICKEN

MARINATES 4 CHICKEN BREAST HALVES

› ½ C. pineapple juice
› 2 T. apricot preserves

› 1 tsp. ground ginger
› 1 tsp. dry mustard

› ½ tsp. salt

In a small bowl, whisk together pineapple juice, preserves, ginger, dry mustard and salt until well blended. Pour mixture over chicken and refrigerate to marinate meat for 3 to 4 hours, turning occasionally. To cook, drain and discard marinade. Grill chicken.

To make Hawaiian Chicken & Pineapple Sandwiches: Spread Thousand Island dressing on split, toasted onion rolls and top each roll with one grilled chicken breast prepared with Tropical Marinade, a grilled pineapple ring and slice of Swiss cheese.

HONEYED TANGERINE GLAZE FOR CHICKEN

MAKES ABOUT ½ CUP

› 3 C. tangerine juice or tangerine-orange juice

› 5 sprigs fresh thyme
› ¼ C. honey

› ½ tsp. salt
› ¼ tsp. black pepper

In a medium saucepan over high heat, combine tangerine juice and thyme. Bring mixture to a boil and cook, stirring frequently, until thickened and reduced to about ½ cup. Remove and discard thyme stems. Whisk in honey until well blended; season with salt and black pepper. Transfer to a bowl and cool glaze to room temperature. To use, grill one side of chicken breast halves (plain or pre-coated with a rub) for 6 to 8 minutes. Turn chicken over and cook for 2 to 3 more minutes. Brush with glaze and continue to cook until almost done. Turn again, brush tops with glaze and finish grilling.

ALL-PURPOSE CHICKEN RUB

MAKES ABOUT ½ CUP

- 3 T. Hungarian paprika*
- 1 T. black pepper
- 1 T. celery salt
- 1 to 2 T. sugar
- 1½ tsp. onion powder
- 1½ tsp. dry mustard
- ½ tsp. cayenne pepper
- 1½ tsp. finely grated lemon peel

In a small bowl, combine paprika, black pepper, celery salt, sugar, onion powder, dry mustard, cayenne pepper and lemon peel; mix well. Refrigerate in an airtight container for up to 5 months. To use, sprinkle mixture on trimmed, uncooked chicken wings and pat mixture evenly over skins. Grill chicken.

* Hungarian paprika is rich and sweet.

TEXAS-STYLE BBQ SAUCE

MAKES ABOUT 2 CUPS

- 1 T. butter
- 1 clove garlic, minced
- 1 C. ketchup
- ⅓ C. brown sugar
- ⅓ C. Worcestershire sauce
- ¼ C. lemon juice
- 1 chipotle chile in adobo sauce, minced with seeds
- ¼ tsp. cayenne pepper
- Salt and black pepper to taste

In a medium saucepan over medium heat, melt butter. Add garlic and sauté for 30 seconds. Stir in ketchup, brown sugar, Worcestershire sauce, lemon juice, chile and cayenne pepper. Bring mixture to a boil, reduce heat and simmer for 15 minutes, stirring occasionally, or until mixture is reduced to 1⅓ cups. Season with salt and black pepper. Cool slightly, cover and chill until needed. Sauce may be brushed on grilled chicken during the last 15 minutes of grilling, or it may be served warm on the side. This sauce also tastes good with grilled chicken tenders.

CITRUS-GARLIC MARINADE FOR TURKEY

MARINATES AND BASTES 4 TURKEY BREAST FILLETS

- ⅓ C. olive oil
- ¼ C. lemon juice
- 1 tsp. finely grated orange peel
- ¼ C. orange juice
- ¼ tsp. salt
- ¼ tsp. black pepper
- 4 cloves garlic, minced

In a small bowl, combine oil, lemon juice, orange peel, orange juice, salt, black pepper and garlic; mix well. Reserve ¼ cup of marinade for basting and refrigerate for later use. Pour remaining marinade over turkey steaks, strips or cubes and refrigerate to marinate turkey for 2 to 4 hours, turning occasionally.

To cook, lightly oil the grate and preheat grill to medium-high heat. Remove turkey and discard marinade. If making kebabs, thread turkey strips or cubes alternately with chunks of fresh vegetables or fruits on metal or soaked wooden skewers. Place turkey or skewers on the grate over medium heat, cover grill and cook for 10 to 15 minutes, turning once, until meat is no longer pink inside and internal temperature reaches 165° to 170°F. Baste turkey with reserved marinade during the last half of grilling time.

ALL-PURPOSE BEEF MARINADE

MARINATES 2 LBS. STEAK

- ¾ C. vegetable oil
- ¼ C. soy sauce
- 1 T. lemon pepper
- 2 tsp. Worcestershire sauce
- 4 to 6 drops hot pepper sauce

In a large resealable plastic bag, combine oil, soy sauce, lemon pepper, Worcestershire sauce, hot pepper sauce and ⅔ cup water; mix well. Add steaks, seal bag and refrigerate to marinate meat for 4 hours or overnight. To cook, remove steak from bag and discard marinade. Grill meat.

SALT-FREE BEEF RUB

MAKES ABOUT ½ CUP

- 2 T. sugar
- 1 tsp. garlic powder
- 1 tsp. cayenne pepper
- ¼ tsp. black pepper
- ½ tsp. white pepper
- 2 tsp. onion powder
- 1 tsp. paprika
- 2 tsp. filé powder
- 2 tsp. dried thyme
- 2½ tsp. dried basil
- ½ tsp. dried oregano

In a small bowl, combine sugar, garlic powder, cayenne pepper, black pepper, white pepper, onion powder, paprika, filé powder, thyme, basil and oregano; mix well. Store in an airtight container and sprinkle or rub on any cut of beef before grilling.

COLA MARINADE FOR BEEF

MARINATES 4 LBS. BEEF RIBS

> 1 C. carbonated cola beverage
> 1½ C. soy sauce
> 2 T. rice wine vinegar

> 1 T. red pepper flakes
> 6 cloves garlic, mashed
> 1 small red onion chopped

In a large resealable plastic bag, mix cola, soy sauce, vinegar, pepper flakes, garlic and onion. Add ribs, seal bag and refrigerate for 24 hours. To cook, lightly oil the grate and preheat grill to medium heat. Discard marinade. Place ribs on the grate, cover grill and cook for 20 to 25 minutes or to desired doneness, turning once. (Ribs may also be cooked over indirect heat for about 1 hour.)

FAR EASTERN RUB FOR PORK

MAKES ABOUT 3 TABLESPOONS

- ❯ 1 T. dry mustard
- ❯ 1½ tsp. ground cumin
- ❯ 1½ tsp. curry powder
- ❯ 1½ tsp. Hungarian paprika
- ❯ ¾ tsp. salt
- ❯ ¼ tsp. cayenne pepper
- ❯ 1 tsp. black pepper
- ❯ ⅛ tsp. ground allspice
- ❯ ⅛ tsp. ground cloves

In a small bowl, combine dry mustard, cumin, curry powder, paprika, salt, cayenne pepper, black pepper, allspice and cloves; mix well. Rub or pat mixture over both sides of pork. Cover and refrigerate for 30 minutes or up to 2 hours. Grill chops.

APPLE CIDER BRINE FOR PORK

BRINES 4 THICK PORK CHOPS

- ½ C. coarse salt (kosher or sea salt)
- ½ C. brown sugar
- 1 tsp. dried thyme
- ½ tsp. whole black peppercorns
- ½ tsp. whole cloves
- 2C. unfiltered apple cider
- 1C. ice cubes
- Olive oil

In a large saucepan over medium heat, mix 1 cup water, salt, brown sugar, thyme, peppercorns and cloves; boil for 2 to 3 minutes until sugar and salt dissolve. Remove from heat; stir in cider and ice. Place pork chops in an extra-large resealable plastic bag. Pour brine over chops, seal bag and refrigerate for 6 to 12 hours. To cook, lightly oil the grate and preheat grill to medium heat. Drain chops, rinse and pat dry; discard brine. Brush with oil and place over direct heat. Cover grill and cook for 12 to 16 minutes, turning once, or until internal temperature reaches 145°F.

PINEAPPLE MARINADE FOR PORK

MARINATES 2 LBS. PORK TENDERLOIN

- ⅓ C. pineapple juice
- 2 T. lime juice
- 2 cloves garlic, minced
- 2 tsp. cumin
- ⅓ C. vegetable oil
- 1 tsp. salt
- ¼ tsp. black pepper

In a large resealable plastic bag, combine pineapple juice, lime juice, garlic, cumin, oil, salt and pepper; mix well. Add tenderloin(s) to the bag, seal and turn to coat. Refrigerate to marinate pork for at least 1 hour or overnight. To cook, remove meat and discard marinade. Lightly oil the grate and preheat grill to medium heat. Place pork on the grate, cover grill and cook for 20 to 25 minutes, turning frequently, until internal temperature reaches 145°F. Remove from heat and let stand 5 minutes under a foil tent before slicing.

ALL-PURPOSE PORK RUB

MAKES ABOUT ¼ CUP

- 1 T. paprika
- 1½ tsp. salt
- 1½ tsp. sugar
- 1½ tsp. brown sugar
- 1½ tsp. ground cumin
- 1½ tsp. chili powder
- 1½ tsp. cayenne pepper
- 1½ tsp. black pepper

In a small bowl, combine paprika, salt, sugar, brown sugar, cumin, chili powder, cayenne pepper and black pepper. Sprinkle mixture over pork roast and rub in well before grilling. Use this rub with any cut of pork.

ROASTED PEPPER SAUCE FOR TUNA OR HALIBUT

GARNISHES 4 TUNA OR HALIBUT STEAKS

- 2 roasted sweet red bell peppers*
- 2 T. lime juice
- 2 tsp. chopped fresh thyme or dillweed
- ¼ tsp. salt
- ⅛ tsp. black pepper
- 1 T. butter

In a blender container or food processor, combine roasted peppers, lime juice, thyme, salt, black pepper and 2 tablespoons water. Cover and blend until smooth. Pour mixture into a small saucepan and cook over low heat until hot; stir in butter until melted. Drizzle warm pepper sauce onto four serving plates and top with grilled tuna or halibut steaks.

To roast, rinse whole peppers and place them on a lightly-oiled grate over medium heat. Grill for 5 to 7 minutes per side, until skins are blistered and browned. Transfer peppers from the grill to an airtight container to steam as they cool. When cool, peel off skins and remove seeds and stem; cut into pieces.

SWEET & SOUR BBQ SAUCE FOR SHRIMP

MAKES ABOUT 3¼ CUPS

- 2 T. olive oil
- 2 T. minced garlic
- 1 C. honey

- ¼ C. soy sauce
- ½ C. balsamic vinegar
- 1 C. ketchup

- ¼ C. fresh brewed coffee
- ½ tsp. vanilla extract

In a medium saucepan over medium-low heat, place oil. Add garlic and cook until golden brown, stirring often. Wisk in honey, soy sauce, vinegar, ketchup and coffee. Simmer for 15 minutes. Stir in vanilla just before serving with grilled shrimp. If desired, reserve ¼ cup of mixture to baste shrimp during grilling.

10 Desserts

There is no better way to bring people together than with desserts.
—*Gail Simmons*

GRILLED APPLE CRISP

MAKES ABOUT 12 SERVINGS

- 10 C. (about 8 medium) thinly sliced, peeled apples
- 1 C. old-fashioned oats
- 1 C. brown sugar
- ¼ C. flour

- 1 T. ground cinnamon
- 1 tsp. ground nutmeg
- ¼ tsp. ground cloves
- ¼ C. cold butter

Place apple slices on a double thickness of heavy-duty aluminum foil (about 12 x 24 inches) which has been sprayed with nonstick cooking spray. In a small bowl, combine oats, brown sugar, flour, cinnamon, nutmeg and cloves; cut in butter until mixture is crumbly. Sprinkle over apples. Fold foil around apple mixture and seal tightly. Grill, covered, over medium heat 20 to 25 minutes or until apples are tender.

GRILLED CHERRY CHOCOLATE PIZZA

SERVINGS VARY

- ½ (8 oz.) tub whipped cream cheese
- 5 T. sugar
- 1 sheet puff pastry, thawed
- Cherry pie filling
- Mini semi-sweet chocolate chips
- Chopped fruit

Preheat grill to medium-high heat. Stir together cream cheese and sugar. Coat a large piece of foil with cooking spray and set on grill rack; unfold pastry on foil. Close grill and cook until bottom is golden brown. Flip crust; spread with cream cheese mixture. Top with pie filling and chocolate chips. Close grill; cook until bottom of crust is golden. Remove from grill and top with fruit.

BERRIES & A POUND

MAKES 6 SERVINGS

- 1 C. whipping cream
- 1 tsp. lemon zest, plus more for sprinkling
- 1 T. lemon juice
- 5 T. sugar, divided
- 1½ C. cubed strawberries
- 1½ C. blueberries
- 1 T. chopped fresh mint
- 1 (10.75 oz.) pkg. frozen pound cake, thawed
- 2 T. softened butter

In a small chilled bowl with chilled beaters, beat cream until it just begins to thicken. Add lemon zest, lemon juice, and 3 tablespoons sugar; beat until soft peaks form. Chill until serving time. Preheat the grill on medium heat. In an 8 x 8-inch foil pan, mix the strawberries, blueberries, mint, and remaining 2 tablespoons sugar. Close the lid and cook until the berries are hot and juicy, about 10 minutes, stirring occasionally. Cut the cake into six slices and spread butter over both cut sides. Set the slices directly on the grill rack and cook a few minutes on each side until golden brown. Serve berries over cake with the chilled whipped cream and sprinkle with more lemon zest.

PUFFED FRUIT TART

MAKES 6 SERVINGS

- ❭ 2 T. cream cheese, softened
- ❭ 2 T. sugar, divided, plus more for sprinkling
- ❭ Flour
- ❭ 1 sheet frozen puff pastry, thawed according to package directions
- ❭ 1 or 2 peaches, pitted & sliced
- ❭ 2 or 3 apricots, pitted & sliced
- ❭ ⅔ C. blueberries
- ❭ Olive oil

Beat together the cream cheese and 1 tablespoon sugar until smooth; set aside. Crumple up aluminum foil to make several 2- to 3-inch diameter balls; set them on the grill rack and set a pizza stone on top of them. Preheat the grill on low to allow the stone to heat up slowly.

Line a cookie sheet with parchment paper; sprinkle with flour and unfold the pastry on top of it. With a knife, score the dough to form a 1-inch border around the outside edges. Sprinkle the border with 1 tablespoon sugar. Using a fork, pierce the dough several times inside the border. Increase the grill temperature to medium. Slide the dough, along with the parchment, onto the hot stone and cook for 15 minutes, until the dough is cooked through, rotating the pan as needed for even cooking. Meanwhile, place the peaches and apricots in a foil pan, put the blueberries in a separate foil pan, and drizzle all the fruit with oil. Put pans on the grill and cook until slightly softened; set aside. Gently spread the set-aside cream cheese mixture inside the border of the pastry and arrange cooked fruit on top. Sprinkle a little more sugar over the fruit, if you'd like.

CARAMEL PINEAPPLE POUND CAKE

MAKES 16 SERVINGS

> 8 oz. cream cheese, softened
> 3 T. brown sugar, plus more to sprinkle
> ⅛ tsp. cinnamon, plus more to sprinkle
> Pineapple

> Brown sugar
> Pound cake
> Caramel ice cream topping, optional
> Pecans, toasted & chopped, optional

Mix cream cheese, brown sugar, and cinnamon; set aside. Line the grill grate with foil, spritz with cooking spray, and preheat the grill on low heat. Core a fresh pineapple and cut into ½-inch-thick rings; sprinkle both sides with brown sugar and cinnamon and arrange rings on the foil. Cut 16 (1 inch thick) slices of pound cake (we used plain and pumpkin-flavored) and set on the foil. Heat everything until grill marks appear on both sides, flipping once. Remove from the grill and spread the set-aside cream cheese mixture over the cake slices. Add a pineapple ring (cut in half if needed), caramel ice cream topping, and toasted chopped pecans.

GRILLED FRUIT PIZZA

MAKES ABOUT 8 SERVINGS

- ½ C. butter, softened
- 1 (8 oz.) pkg. cream cheese, softened
- ¾ C. powdered sugar
- 1 tsp. almond extract
- 1 T. honey

- 1 (13.8 oz.) can refrigerated pizza crust dough
- 4½ C. fruit (strawberries, kiwifruit, grapes and mandarin oranges work great)

Preheat grill to medium heat. In a medium mixing bowl, combine butter, cream cheese, sugar and almond extract. Beat with hand mixer on low speed until smooth and creamy; set aside. In a small bowl, combine honey and 1 tablespoon water, stirring until honey dissolves; set aside. Unroll pizza dough and place on oiled grate. Grill for about 4 minutes on each side. Brush with honey mixture and grill an additional 2 minutes. Remove from grill and spread with cream cheese mixture. Top with fruit.

CINNAMON FLAT ROLLS

MAKES ABOUT 6 SERVINGS

- ¼ C. sugar
- 1½ tsp. ground cinnamon
- 6 frozen white dinner rolls, thawed
- 2 T. olive oil, divided

Preheat grill to medium heat. In a small bowl, combine sugar and cinnamon; set aside. On a floured surface, flatten each dinner roll into a 5 inches round. Brush one side with oil. Grill, oil side down, uncovered, 1 minute or until golden brown, bursting any large bubbles with a fork. Turn roll over, brush with oil and sprinkle with cinnamon-sugar mixture. Grill until golden brown.

CAMPFIRE BAKED FRUIT

MAKES 4 SERVINGS

- 4 apples or pears
- ½ C. dried fruits
- ½ C. shredded coconut
- 1 tsp. ground cinnamon
- ½ C. sugar
- 2 tsp. butter, softened

Core whole fruit to form a cavity; fill with dried fruits and coconut, packing it fairly tight. Mix cinnamon and sugar. Sprinkle each filled cavity with ½ teaspoon cinnamon-sugar mixture and ½ teaspoon butter. Preheat grill to medium heat. Set fruit cored-side-up on heavy-duty aluminum foil. Add 1 teaspoon butter and a sprinkle of cinnamon and sugar to each cavity or stuff with filling. To grill, wrap securely in aluminum foil, folding ends over, leaving a little space for air circulation. Grill, seam side up, about 10 minutes or until fruit is slightly tender.

FRUIT 'N' CAKE KEBABS

MAKES 8 SERVINGS

- ½ C. apricot preserves
- 1 T. butter
- ⅛ tsp. ground cinnamon
- ⅛ tsp. ground nutmeg
- 3 nectarines, pitted and quartered
- 6 medium apricots, pitted and halved
- 3 medium peaches, pitted and quartered
- 1 (10.75 oz.) loaf frozen pound cake, thawed and cut into 2" cubes

Preheat grill to medium heat. In a small saucepan over medium heat, blend preserves, 1 tablespoon water, butter, cinnamon and nutmeg. On eight skewers, alternately thread fruit and cake. Grill, uncovered, for 1 to 2 minutes on each side or until cake is golden and fruit is tender, brushing often with apricot mixture.

FRUIT & CHOCOLATE SAUCE

MAKES 6 SERVINGS

- ¾ C. semi-sweet chocolate chips
- ¼ C. butter
- ⅔ C. sugar
- 1 (5 oz.) can evaporated milk

- 2 peaches, pitted and cut into wedges
- 2 bananas, peeled and cut into 1" chunks
- 6 strawberries, stemmed
- Large marshmallows, optional

In a small saucepan over low heat, melt chocolate and butter. Add sugar. Gradually stir in milk. Bring to a boil; reduce heat and cook, stirring constantly, about 8 minutes. Set aside. Preheat grill to medium heat. Alternately thread fruit and marshmallows onto skewers*. Grill for about 5 minutes, turning once. Remove from grill and serve with warm chocolate sauce.

If using wooden skewers, be sure to soak in water at least 30 minutes to prevent burning.

BANANA BLISS

MAKES 4 SERVINGS

- 2 ripe bananas, unpeeled
- 2 C. miniature marshmallows
- 2 C. semisweet chocolate chips
- Brown sugar

Leaving the peel on, slit the bananas lengthwise, but not all the way through the peel. Put half of the marshmallows and chocolate chips in the slit of each banana. Lightly sprinkle brown sugar on top of each banana. Wrap each banana tightly in foil, making sure to seal ends. Place on a medium-hot grill, seam side up, for about 7 minutes. Carefully remove bananas from grill; place in serving dish; unwrap; and serve hot.

CHOCOLATE BANANA PEANUT BUTTER CUPS

MAKES 4 SERVINGS

› 4 miniature graham cracker pie crusts
› 1 banana

› 12 miniature peanut butter cup candies
› Marshmallows, toasted

Preheat grill to medium heat. Place pie crusts in a disposable foil pan. Peel and slice banana, and layer 3 to 4 slices in each pie crust. Place 3 peanut butter cups over top of bananas. Uncover and place a few toasted marshmallows on top of each, and serve.

APPLE TORTILLA STRUDEL

EACH PACK SERVES 1–2

- ❯ 1 10" flour tortilla
- ❯ 1½ T. sliced butter
- ❯ ½ C. diced apple
- ❯ 1 T. brown sugar
- ❯ Cinnamon
- ❯ 2 T. chopped pecans
- ❯ 2 T. granola cereal

For each strudel, set 1 (10-inch) flour tortilla on a large piece of sprayed foil. Arrange 1½ tablespoons. sliced butter across the center and layer with ½ cup diced apple, 1 tablespoon brown sugar, some cinnamon, and 2 tablespoons each chopped pecans and granola cereal. (Try other combos like peanut butter, diced apple, brown sugar, peanuts, and chocolate chips.) Roll up the tortilla burrito-style, folding ends in to keep filling inside. Place seam side down on foil and wrap to make a flat pack. Cook as directed until apples are tender.

To grill, set foil pack(s) on the grate over medium heat and cover grill. Cook 10 to 15 minutes, flipping over once.

CHERRY-COCONUT CRISP

SERVES 4

- ½ C. quick-cooking oats
- ⅓ C. raw chip or shredded coconut
- ¼ C. chopped pecans or walnuts
- 3 T. sugar, divided
- ½ tsp. ground cinnamon, or more to taste
- 1½ T. canola oil
- 1½ T. pure maple syrup
- 1 (12 oz.) pkg. frozen dark sweet cherries, thawed
- 1 T. lemon juice
- 1 T. cornstarch
- 4 canned pineapple slices, drained
- Chocolate chips

In a small bowl, combine oats, coconut, pecans, 2 tablespoons sugar, and cinnamon. Stir in oil and syrup and set aside. In a large bowl, combine cherries, remaining 1 tablespoon sugar, lemon juice, and cornstarch; toss well. Place one pineapple slice on each of four pieces of sprayed foil. Spoon cherry mixture evenly over pineapple and top each with part of the oat mixture. Sprinkle with a few chocolate chips, if desired. Wrap foil around food to make four tent packs and cook as directed. Set foil packs on the grate over medium heat and cook 12 to 14 minutes or until hot.

PUMPKIN MUFFINS

MAKES 16 MUFFINS

> 8 large oranges
> 1 (14 oz.) package Pumpkin Quick Bread & Muffin Mix
> (with water, oil, and eggs as directed on package)

Cut 8 large oranges in half and scoop out the flesh to make 16 shells. In a bowl, mix 1 (14 oz.) pkg. Pumpkin Quick Bread & Muffin Mix with water, oil, and eggs as directed on the package. Fill each orange shell halfway with batter (you may have extra). Wrap shells individually in sprayed foil to make 16 tent packs and cook as directed until muffins test done with a toothpick.

To grill, set foil packs on the grate over medium heat (batter side up) and cover grill. Cook 10 to 15 minutes.

EASY GRILLED DONUT SHORTCAKES

MAKES 8 SERVINGS

- ¼ C. sugar
- 1 T. cinnamon
- ¼ C. melted butter
- 2 T. brown sugar

- 16 oz. tube jumbo refrigerated buttermilk biscuits
- Whipped cream
- Fresh fruit, chopped

Line the grill grate with foil and spritz with cooking spray. Preheat the grill on low heat. In a bowl, stir together sugar and cinnamon. In a separate bowl, mix the butter with brown sugar. Set both aside. Separate the biscuits from the tube; push a hole through the center of each biscuit. Arrange the biscuits on the foil. Close the grill lid and cook 4 to 5 minutes on each side, until browned on the outside and cooked through. Remove the biscuits from the grill; one at a time, dip both sides in the butter mixture and toss around in the cinnamon-sugar to coat. Top with spray whipped cream and pile on the fresh fruit.

INDEX